Kogun

33 1/3 Global

33 1/3 Global, a series related to but independent from **33 1/3**, takes the format of the original series of short, music-based books and brings the focus to music throughout the world. With initial volumes focusing on Japanese and Brazilian music, the series will also include volumes on the popular music of Australia/Oceania, Europe, Africa, the Middle East, and more.

33 1/3 Japan
Series Editor: Noriko Manabe
Spanning a range of artists and genres—from the 1970s rock of Happy End to technopop band Yellow Magic Orchestra, the Shibuya-kei of Cornelius, classic anime series *Cowboy Bebop*, J-Pop/EDM hybrid Perfume, and vocaloid star Hatsune Miku—**33 1/3 Japan** is a series devoted to in-depth examination of Japanese popular music of the twentieth and twenty-first centuries.

Published Titles:
Supercell's *Supercell* by Keisuke Yamada
AKB48 by Patrick W. Galbraith and Jason G. Karlin
Yoko Kanno's *Cowboy Bebop Soundtrack* by Rose Bridges
Perfume's *Game* by Patrick St. Michel
Cornelius's *Fantasma* by Martin Roberts
Joe Hisaishi's *My Neighbor Totoro: Soundtrack* by Kunio Hara
Shonen Knife's *Happy Hour* by Brooke McCorkle
Nenes' *Koza Dabasa* by Henry Johnson
Yuming's *The 14th Moon* by Lasse Lehtonen
Toshiko Akiyoshi-Lew Tabackin Big Band's *Kogun* by E. Taylor Atkins

Forthcoming Titles:
Yellow Magic Orchestra's *Yellow Magic Orchestra* by Toshiyuki Ohwada
Kohaku utagassen: The Red and White Song Contest by Shelley Brunt
S.O.B.'s *Don't Be Swindle* by Mahon Murphy and Ran Zwigenberg

33 1/3 Brazil
Series Editor: Jason Stanyek
Covering the genres of samba, tropicália, rock, hip hop, forró, bossa nova, heavy metal and funk, among others, **33 1/3 Brazil** is a series devoted to in-depth examination of the most important Brazilian albums of the twentieth and twenty-first centuries.

Published Titles:
Caetano Veloso's *A Foreign Sound* by Barbara Browning
Tim Maia's *Tim Maia Racional Vols. 1 & 2* by Allen Thayer
João Gilberto and Stan Getz's *Getz/Gilberto* by Brian McCann
Gilberto Gil's *Refazenda* by Marc A. Hertzman
Dona Ivone Lara's *Sorriso Negro* by Mila Burns
Milton Nascimento and Lô Borges's *The Corner Club* by Jonathon Grasse
Racionais MCs' *Sobrevivendo no Inferno* by Derek Pardue
Naná Vasconcelos's *Saudades* by Daniel B. Sharp
Chico Buarque's First *Chico Buarque* by Charles A. Perrone

Forthcoming titles:
Jorge Ben Jor's *África Brasil* by Frederick J. Moehn

33 1/3 Europe
Series Editor: Fabian Holt
Spanning a range of artists and genres, **33 1/3 Europe** offers engaging accounts of popular and culturally significant albums of Continental Europe and the North Atlantic from the twentieth and twenty-first centuries.

Published Titles:
Darkthrone's *A Blaze in the Northern Sky* by Ross Hagen
Ivo Papazov's *Balkanology* by Carol Silverman
Heiner Müller and Heiner Goebbels's *Wolokolamsker Chaussee* by Philip V. Bohlman

Modeselektor's *Happy Birthday!* by Sean Nye
Mercyful Fate's *Don't Break the Oath* by Henrik Marstal
Bea Playa's *I'll Be Your Plaything* by Anna Szemere and András Rónai
Various Artists' *DJs do Guetto* by Richard Elliott
Czesław Niemen's *Niemen Enigmatic* by Ewa Mazierska and Mariusz Gradowski
Massada's *Astaganaga* by Lutgard Mutsaers
Los Rodriguez's *Sin Documentos* by Fernán del Val and Héctor Fouce
Édith Piaf's *Récital 1961* by David Looseley
Nuovo Canzoniere Italiano's *Bella Ciao* by Jacopo Tomatis
Iannis Xenakis's *Persepolis* by Aram Yardumian
Vopli Vidopliassova's *Tantsi* by Maria Sonevytsky
Amália Rodrigues's *Amália at the Olympia* by Lila Ellen Gray
Ardit Gjebrea's *Projekt Jon* by Nicholas Tochka
Aqua's *Aquarium* by C.C. McKee
Einstürzende Neubauten's *Kollaps* by Melle Jan Kromhout and Jan Nieuwenhuis

Forthcoming Titles:
J.M.K.E.'s *To the Cold Land* by Brigitta Davidjants
Taco Hemingway's *Jarmark* by Kamila Rymajdo
Tripes' *Kefali Gemato Hrisafi* by Dafni Tragaki
Silly's *Februar* by Michael Rauhut
CCCP's *Fedeli Alla Linea's 1964–1985 Affinità-Divergenze Fra Il Compagno Togliatti E Noi Del Conseguimento Della Maggiore Età* by Giacomo Bottà
Sigur Rós' *Ágætis Byrjun* by Tore Størvold

33 1/3 Oceania

Series Editors: Jon Stratton (senior editor) and Jon Dale (specializing in books on albums from Aotearoa/New Zealand)

Spanning a range of artists and genres from Australian Indigenous artists to Maori and Pasifika artists, from Aotearoa/New Zealand noise music to Australian rock, and including music from Papua and other Pacific islands, **33 1/3 Oceania** offers exciting accounts of albums that illustrate the wide range of music made in the Oceania region.

Published Titles:
John Farnham's *Whispering Jack* by Graeme Turner
The Church's *Starfish* by Chris Gibson
Regurgitator's *Unit* by Lachlan Goold and Lauren Istvandity
Kylie Minogue's *Kylie* by Adrian Renzo and Liz Giuffre
Alastair Riddell's *Space Waltz* by Ian Chapman
Hunters & Collectors's *Human Frailty* by Jon Stratton
The Front Lawn's *Songs from the Front Lawn* by Matthew Bannister
Bic Runga's *Drive* by Henry Johnson
The Dead C's *Clyma est mort* by Darren Jorgensen
Ed Kuepper's *Honey Steel's Gold* by John Encarnacao
Chain's *Toward the Blues* by Peter Beilharz
Hilltop Hoods' *The Calling* by Dianne Rodger
Screamfeeder's *Kitten Licks* by Ben Green and Ian Rogers
Soundtrack from *Saturday Night Fever* by Clinton Walker

Forthcoming Titles:
The Triffids' *Born Sandy Devotional* by Christina Ballico
Crowded House's *Together Alone* by Barnaby Smith
5MMM's *Compilation Album of Adelaide Bands 1980* by Collette Snowden
The Clean's *Boodle Boodle Boodle* by Geoff Stahl
INXS' *Kick* by Ryan Daniel and Lauren Moxey
Sunnyboys' *Sunnyboys* by Stephen Bruel
Eyeliner's *Buy Now* by Michael Brown
Silverchair's *Frogstomp* by Jay Daniel Thompson
TISM's *Machiavelli and the Four Seasons* by Tyler Jenke
The La De Das' *The Happy Prince* by John Tebbutt
John Sangster's *Lord of the Rings Suite* by Bruce Johnson
Gary Shearston's *Dingo* by Peter Mills
The Avalanches' *Since I Left You* by Charles Fairchild

Kogun

E. Taylor Atkins

Series Editor: Noriko Manabe

BLOOMSBURY ACADEMIC
NEW YORK • LONDON • OXFORD • NEW DELHI • SYDNEY

BLOOMSBURY ACADEMIC
Bloomsbury Publishing Inc
1385 Broadway, New York, NY 10018, USA
50 Bedford Square, London, WC1B 3DP, UK
29 Earlsfort Terrace, Dublin 2, Ireland

BLOOMSBURY, BLOOMSBURY ACADEMIC and the Diana logo are trademarks of Bloomsbury Publishing Plc

First published in the United States of America 2024

Copyright © E. Taylor Atkins, 2024

For legal purposes the Acknowledgments on p.xii constitute an extension of this copyright page.

All rights reserved. No part of this publication may be reproduced or transmitted in any form or by any means, electronic or mechanical, including photocopying, recording, or any information storage or retrieval system, without prior permission in writing from the publishers.

Bloomsbury Publishing Inc does not have any control over, or responsibility for, any third-party websites referred to or in this book. All internet addresses given in this book were correct at the time of going to press. The author and publisher regret any inconvenience caused if addresses have changed or sites have ceased to exist, but can accept no responsibility for any such changes.

Whilst every effort has been made to locate copyright holders the publishers would be grateful to hear from any person(s) not here acknowledged.

A catalog record for this book is available from the Library of Congress.

ISBN: HB: 979-8-7651-0900-7
PB: 979-8-7651-0901-4
ePDF: 979-8-7651-0903-8
eBook: 979-8-7651-0902-1

Typeset by Deanta Global Publishing Services, Chennai, India

Series: 33 1/3 Japan

To find out more about our authors and books visit www.bloomsbury.com and sign up for our newsletters.

*For the Sugiuras,
my Japanese family*

Contents

Acknowledgments xii

Introduction 1

1 **The Lone Soldier** 9

2 **The Long Yellow Road** 25

3 **The Band** 43

4 **The Record** 57

5 **The Title Track** 67

6 **The Reckoning** 99

Epilogue: The Legacy 111

Notes 121
References 126
Index 137

Acknowledgments

My first word of thanks goes to Noriko Manabe, a scholar whose work I greatly admire, for inviting me to contribute something to the 33 1/3 Japan series and shepherding the proposal so carefully. I never considered writing about anything but *Kogun*. This is my second book with Bloomsbury, and, again, it's been a wonderful experience. Leah Babb-Rosenfeld and all the folks at the press have been a joy to work with.

I had the honor of meeting Toshiko Akiyoshi and Lew Tabackin in August 1994, when I accompanied jazz historian Segawa Masahisa to a performance by their orchestra at NHK Studios in Tokyo. I had an enjoyable visit with Mr. Tabackin over lunch in the cafeteria before the show. I later interviewed Ms. Akiyoshi briefly by phone in February 1996. I was delighted to have another opportunity to meet them when Mr. Tabackin agreed to an interview in January 2023. Ms. Akiyoshi didn't join us ("She just doesn't like to do this stuff. It takes too much energy," he said), but answered some questions through him. I hope this book does them and their music justice—and helps get it back in print!

Many thanks as well to: Bobby Shew and Mike Price for granting me interviews; Kevin Fellezs and the participants of the February 2023 Asian/American Jazz Symposium at the Center for Jazz Studies at Columbia University for much-needed encouragement and validation; Ayako Yoshimura,

East Asia librarian at the University of Chicago; and my NIU colleagues Damián Fernández, Sean Farrell, Aaron Fogleman, Valerie Garver, Amanda Littauer, Ismael Montana, and Jui-Ching Wang for their helpful feedback and support. I am most grateful to you all.

My wife, Carolyn, has shared my enthusiasm for this project and never fails to support me in everything I do (unless it's a bad idea). I adore you, darling.

I dedicate this book with gratitude to the Sugiura family in Okazaki, fellow jazzheads who are not only among my dearest friends but also family. They have shown me what it's like to live with genuine joy. この著書を、私の親愛なる友人であるとともに、家族のような存在でもあり、また同じ「ジャズクレージー」として大切な仲間でもある、愛知県岡崎市の杉浦家の皆様に感謝を込めて捧げます。私に生きる喜びを教えて下さいました。

Japanese transliteration follows the Hepburn system. East Asian names are rendered surnames first, except for Toshiko Akiyoshi and others who use reverse order professionally.

Introduction

In March 1974, Toshiko Akiyoshi was on the verge of reinventing herself and reinvigorating her career as a jazz artist. For almost two decades since she arrived in the United States from Japan with a scholarship to the Berklee School of Music in Boston, she had become one of the most respected bebop pianists in the scene. She led trios with some of the best bassists and drummers in the business: Paul Chambers, Ed Thigpen, Oscar Pettiford, Roy Haynes, Ron Carter, and Mickey Roker. She twice held the piano chair in Charles Mingus' band. She had also shown ambition as a composer, writing challenging yet memorably melodious pieces such as "Long Yellow Road" and "The Village," a song with a daunting left-hand ostinato in 5/4 (well, actually, 15/8) that she played continuously while improvising with her right.[1]

But by the mid-1960s, Akiyoshi was at a crossroads. In 1965, she and her husband, alto saxophonist Charlie Mariano (1923–2009), returned to the United States from a demoralizing two-year sojourn in Japan, trying to elevate a jazz scene that she said lacked "guts" (Atkins 2001, 212–13). Soon she was raising their daughter, Monday Michiru, alone and planning to study computer programming. She wondered if she had any business playing jazz and was prepared to quit. If she could contribute nothing distinctive and valuable to the art she so dearly loved, it would not be worth such economic hardship.

She would likely be a footnote in jazz history: the "Japanese little girl" (her words) who momentarily jammed with giants, an exotic curiosity.

"I really had to take a look at who I was and what I was trying to do," she later reflected.

> At least if you're an American it's *justified*, let's say, to be a jazz musician. Jazz is American music. And I thought, here I am, I'm a Japanese and a woman . . . and playing in New York. I never thought I was a bad player, but there are so many great players, too. And I look at it and then have to really think about where my position is, what my role will be. And somehow it looks kind of pathetic and comical, the fact that there is a Japanese little girl trying to play jazz . . . and I felt very insignificant. Did I do something, did I make any kind of revolution [in] the jazz world? At that time, I thought to take that opportunity to just become a nice little woman who cleans the house and cooks. (Cho 1983)

She often spoke in terms of obligation, of having "reaped the benefits" of jazz without offering anything in return (Feather 1976, 16; Akiyoshi 1979b). However, she had become more confident that her Japanese background, which, despite its occasional novelty value, she considered a liability, could be an asset, a resource for contributing something original and distinctive to the jazz corpus. Her second husband, tenor saxophonist and flutist Lew Tabackin, believed in her talents and urged her to stay in the game (Atkins 2001, 240–1; Akiyoshi 1996, 208–9).

In May 1972, Tabackin's job in Doc Severinsen's band on *The Tonight Show with Johnny Carson* required the couple to relocate to Los Angeles. Still unsure about whether to continue her musical career, Akiyoshi and Tabackin assembled a rehearsal band of studio aces who devoted hours of unpaid time each week to learning her compositions and arrangements for jazz orchestra. The enthusiasm these musicians showed for her work was encouraging enough that Akiyoshi discussed recording an album with a producer at RCA/Victor Japan. Studio time was booked for April 1974.

In early March, Akiyoshi saw on television the news that would change her career and, by extension, the history of jazz music. A slender man wearing the tattered remains of his Japanese military uniform emerged from the jungle and surrendered to police in the Philippines, where he had been waging a small-scale guerrilla campaign for almost thirty years after the end of the Pacific War. Those three decades coincided precisely with Akiyoshi's own "long yellow road" toward a seat of honor in the jazz pantheon.

* * *

This book argues that the 1974 album *Kogun* deserves recognition as a landmark in jazz history. It launched the distinguished (second) career of one of the most acclaimed composers in modern jazz and introduced several of the innovative, signature stylistic elements of her work. It revived the artistic vitality of the big band at a time when that format was disparaged and unpopular. It elevated the status of and opened opportunities for women in the jazz idiom while also expanding the music's sonic vocabulary and cosmopolitanism. The title track of *Kogun* addressed Japan's wartime experiences and legacies in musical language, presaging later Akiyoshi compositions that evoked and commented on some of the most pivotal and traumatic moments in modern Japanese history.

Kogun was released at a time when big bands were considered primarily vehicles for Swing-Era nostalgia, and the fusion of jazz with rock and funk had started to dominate listeners' attention and the market. Whereas musicians and critics who led the 1980s' neo-classicist "jazz renaissance" routinely derided and dismissed the 1970s as a decade of artistic impoverishment and "selling out," *Kogun* and subsequent albums by the Akiyoshi-Tabackin orchestra indicated not only the jazz idiom's creative vitality in that decade but also the continuing relevance and promise of the big-band medium.

Kogun was also a milestone for female jazz musicians, as well as for artists whose heritage was outside of the United States and the African diaspora. Following in the footsteps of respected composer/arranger/instrumentalists such as Mary Lou Williams and Melba Liston, Akiyoshi was one of very few female leaders of an all-male ensemble and the first to helm a jazz orchestra devoted to playing her own original compositions and arrangements, as had the respective bands of Duke Ellington, Charles Mingus, and Sun Ra. Concurrently with Carla Bley, she paved the way for Maria Schneider, Fujii Satoko, Amina Figarova, Hazama Miho, Jill Townsend, and Christine Jensen to rise to the elite ranks of jazz composers and orchestra leaders, and for countless other women to be taken seriously as instrumentalists in jazz, which has been called "the most macho of all arts" (Gourse 1995, 7).

Before Toshiko Akiyoshi burst onto the American jazz scene in the late 1950s as a talented bebop pianist, very few non-Americans had achieved recognition as major innovators in the idiom. Although partially based on the string-band jazz of violinist Joe Venuti and guitarist Eddie Lang, Django Reinhardt and Stéphane Grappelli's *jazz manouche* ("gypsy jazz") came to be regarded as a distinctive stylistic contribution, as had the Afro-Caribbean music of Cuban-born artists Mario Bauzá, Machito, and Chano Pozo, and the bossa nova of Brazilians João Gilberto and Antônio Carlos Jobim. There were few others.

In her efforts to create a unique voice, Akiyoshi intentionally, but with artful restraint, introduced identifiably Japanese elements into her orchestrations, expanding further jazz's sonic palette and engagement with musical traditions apart from the genre's African and European inputs. Kevin Fellezs (2010) aptly describes her music as "rootless but not route-less," in that she turned her "demographically challenged" status to her creative advantage, "allow[ing] her the freedom to enlist elements from distant cultures in her work as blends or infusions without having to adhere to conventional notions of cultural legitimacy" (53, 55). As the first major expression of this "rootless" aesthetic, *Kogun* was thus a milestone in the development of a more cosmopolitan jazz aesthetic, what some call "world jazz" (Gioia 2021, 322, 422, 440; Bohlman and Plastino 2016).

Finally, the album was released at a moment when Japanese were beginning to reckon with their imperial and wartime past on a scale and with a candor not seen since the US military occupation that followed the Second World War (1945–52). Japanese have long been criticized for failing to honestly address and express genuine contrition for the brutality of their imperial rule and military conduct in Pacific Asia. Compared to the example of postwar Germany, where the Nazi past has been officially (if fitfully) discredited and concrete efforts made to reconcile and recompense, many find Japan's high-level government responses inadequate and insincere (Buruma 1994; Seaton 2007).

Japan's former adversary encouraged obfuscation and indifference to the wartime past. Intent on rehabilitating Japan as a staunch anti-communist ally during the Cold War, US Occupation officials suppressed information, rehabilitated convicted war criminals, and protected Emperor Hirohito from prosecution for war crimes, among other things. Since then, however, despite their government's reticence to take responsibility without equivocation or offer reparations, thousands of ordinary Japanese have pursued an honest accounting of the imperial state's many atrocities, sometimes at great professional and personal risk. Their efforts have helped instigate waves of public remembrance; they have also provoked hostile, virulent denial.

One moment of reckoning occurred in the early 1970s, initiated in part by the publication by journalist/activist Honda Katsuichi (b. 1933) of first-hand survivor testimonies of the mass rapes and butchery that the Imperial Japanese Army committed in the Chinese capital, Nanjing, in December 1937 (Honda 1972, 1999). This coincided with the discovery of three soldiers on several islands in the Pacific Ocean, as well as the release of *Kogun*.

While it was no celebration of militarism or *bushidō*, its title track nonetheless was a sympathetic acknowledgment of the endurance and suffering of men who had been declared dead and separated from their families and communities for three decades, fighting a war that was long over. They had been indoctrinated in the ideology of imperial divinity and in strict obedience to their superior officers. "Kogun" thus participated in the reckoning with Japan's wartime past.

In this respect, Akiyoshi was partially inspired by her former mentor and bandleader Charles Mingus, whose music often addressed racial politics and other social issues (e.g., "Fables of Faubus," "Meditations on Integration"), and by Duke Ellington's musical narrations of African American history (the 1941 *Jump for Joy* revue and the 1943 *Black, Brown and Beige* suite). "Kogun" was the first of her programmatic compositions for jazz orchestra intended to inspire critical reflection on extramusical matters, establishing Akiyoshi's voice as a historian whose collective works constitute a powerful counter-narrative to the triumphalist account of modern Japanese history.

1 The Lone Soldier

Lt. Onoda Hiroo, Fourteenth Area Army, Eighth Division (Sugi Brigade), Imperial Japanese Army (IJA), was declared dead in December 1959. His last known whereabouts were on Lubang, an island in the Philippine archipelago just southwest of Luzon, where he had arrived on December 26, 1944, with orders to monitor Allied troop movements and carry out guerrilla activities. After US and Philippine Commonwealth forces retook Lubang on February 28, 1945, and decimated his unit, Onoda and his comrades, Cpl. Shimada Shōichi, Pvt. Akatsu Yūichi, and Pvt. Kozuka Kinshichi melted into the jungle.

Throughout the 1950s, Japanese authorities had reason to suspect the soldiers were still alive. In 1959, the Japanese Ministry of Health and Welfare embarked on a six-month campaign to reestablish contact with them, dropping personalized leaflets from airplanes that addressed the soldiers by name, urging them to surrender to local police rather than shoot at them, and to return to their families in Japan.

The leaflets bore the unthinkable news that the Japanese empire was no more, that the emperor had surrendered to the Allies, and that the "holy war" to liberate Asia from Western imperialism and spread the "imperial way" to "the eight corners of the earth" had ended in ignominious failure. The "smashing of the jewels" (*ichioku gyokusai*)—a euphemism for a mass suicidal effort by the Japanese people to defend their homeland with bamboo spears and rice pots—had not transpired. For the first time in its history, Japan had been occupied and governed by foreign troops. It had rejected militarism and fascism and embraced democracy. The emperor had renounced his divinity. The leaflets included photographic evidence of all of this. Akatsu, who had deserted and surrendered in 1950, left a letter testifying that it was all true.

When one considers the indoctrination Onoda and his squad had undergone their entire lives, one can understand why they found such news preposterous. Japan was "the land of the gods" under the care of the divine heir to history's oldest surviving monarchy, its people known for their hardiness, loyalty, perseverance, and fierce determination to die in service to the emperor and nation. Japan was indomitable, divinely anointed and protected, and the moral exemplar for all nations. Defeat at the hands of the materialistic, individualistic, and imperialistic Anglo-American bullies beggared belief. Hadn't the Allies used this propaganda tactic before (as had the Japanese military), dropping on the enemy leaflets packed with verbal and visual lies, trying to deceive them into capitulation and break their spirits?

Onoda, a graduate of the elite Nakano School for military intelligence officers, was naturally suspicious and knew better than to underestimate the enemy. It was not inconceivable that his clever nemeses had learned his identity from Akatsu and slyly attempted to lure him out with personalized entreaties. He was having none of it.

* * *

Onoda Hiroo (1922–2014) was from Kamekawa, a village in modern-day Kainan City, Wakayama prefecture. Before enlisting in the IJA at age eighteen, he had worked for a trading company in Hankou (now part of Wuhan), China, a country with which Japan was then at war. Unlike most other Japanese, he mingled enough with locals to learn passable Chinese.

His other aptitude was for music. A self-described "playboy" who "could dance all night," he frequented the dance halls in Hankou's French Concession until he was shamed out of the habit by local Japanese-language newspapers that "began to call those of us who frequented the French Concession the 'vermin of Asia.'" Commercial ballrooms were among the most closely monitored and tightly regulated entertainment enterprises in Japan, the inspiration for near-constant moral panic in the interwar period. Critics accused dance halls and the jazz music performed in them—which would be officially labeled "enemy music" (*tekisei ongaku*) in the 1940s—of disrupting or disturbing public morality and traditional customs. Eventually, on October 31, 1940, the Home Ministry closed all ballrooms in Japan. Thousands of miles away, demonstrating the upright stoicism for which he would become renowned, Onoda Hiroo abstained of his own volition and focused his musical interests on learning to sing "mostly blues and tangos" from recordings (Onoda 1974, 20–1, 82–3; see also Toi 2005).

Onoda enlisted in the IJA in 1942 and was deployed to Nanchang, China. In 1944, he was selected for commando training at the Futamata branch of the Nakano School, a training facility for military intelligence officers. Because he and his classmates were to be instructed in "secret warfare" (*mitsusen*), the commander advised them that the school's name and existence were top secret. Accordingly, they were "to discard any ideas you may have had of achieving military honors" (Onoda 1974, 29). If their missions were successful, no one would know.

Futamata students had to be deprogrammed from their prior military training and learn "a whole new concept of war." They had aspired to lead men into battle, not engage in "underhanded techniques." "The attack drills at the officers' training school had been lessons in open warfare, which is fundamentally unicellular," Onoda reflected. "We were now being taught a multicellular type of warfare in which every available particle of information is used to throw the enemy into confusion." It was a more "liberal education," in which cadets "were encouraged to think for ourselves." "I liked this," Onoda recalled. "This kind of training and this kind of warfare seemed to suit my personality." His commanders insisted it was an honor to be selected for such training.[1] "I, for one, was at least happy to be told that I had a good brain" (Onoda 1974, 30–3).

Another departure from standard military doctrine was that it was "permissible" for intelligence officers to be taken prisoner. Being captured alive by the enemy was a tremendous dishonor for a Japanese soldier and his whole family. Chapter 2, Article 8 of the Field Service Code (*Senjinkun*) could not have been more explicit:

> Meet the expectations of your family and home community by making effort upon effort, always mindful of the honour

of your name. If alive, do not suffer the disgrace of becoming a prisoner; in death, do not leave behind a name soiled by misdeeds. (Rikugunshō 1941, 13)

At Futamata, however, "By becoming prisoners, we were told, we would place ourselves in a position to give the enemy false information. Indeed, there might be times when we ought deliberately to let ourselves be captured. . . . In short, the lesson was that the end justifies the means" (even medieval samurai seldom let little things like honor and integrity stand in the way of military expediency). Futamata cadets had to be persuaded that "In secret warfare, there is integrity." If captured by the enemy, "we would not be held liable by the army." The downside was that "Only insiders . . . would ever know that we had been engaged in secret warfare, and would have to face the taunts of outsiders as best we could" (Onoda 1974, 33–4).

Ironically, when Onoda returned to visit his family before reporting for duty, his mother gave him an heirloom dagger with which she instructed him to kill himself if he were captured. "I nodded, but inside I knew that I was not going to commit suicide even if I were taken captive. To do so would be a violation of my duty as a secret warfare agent." Given the nature of his work, he told her that she should be skeptical of any report of his death. "I may well show up again after a few years" (Onoda 1974, 37–8).

* * *

Onoda and his mates were among a group of soldiers sizable and prominent enough to be labeled: *zanryū nipponhei*, "Japanese soldiers left behind." However, Onoda was "atypical" of that group. Most such castaways were aware that the war had ended unfavorably for Japan and had simply elected to stay in their respective locations for a variety of reasons (thousands more did *not* stay voluntarily) (Hayashi 2014, 4–5). Some believed there was nothing for which to return. Others, motivated by the pan-Asian idealism that provided an altruistic pretext for Japan's imperialist expansion, joined independence armies in Indochina and Indonesia to resist the reimposition of French and Dutch colonial rule. Japanese soldiers also participated in the Chinese Civil War (1945–9) that ended with a communist victory (Goto 2003, chapter 8, 272–4, 278, 283; Hayashi 2014, chapter 4).

Nonetheless, the ones who emerged decades after the war was over, either unaware or unconvinced of its outcome, were the main objects of public fascination both within and outside Japan. Between 1945 and 1960, several individuals and full or partial units were discovered in Iwo Jima, Dutch New Guinea, the Marianas, and several Philippine islands (Yamakage and Matsudo 1968). Yet only a few became household names in Japan and figures of interest in the foreign press: Sgt. Yokoi Shōichi (1915–97), a holdout in Guam until 1972; Onoda; and Pvt. Nakamura Teruo (née Suniyon, 1918–79), an Amis/Pangcah aborigine from Taiwan who came out of hiding on Morotai island, Indonesia, nine months after Onoda's surrender (Satō 1987; Hayashi 2014, 20–2).[2]

Timing may be one reason these three garnered so much attention. They repatriated at a time when Japanese were fitfully beginning to address in public some painful legacies of the empire and war that had been "forgotten"—quite willfully, by some—or deliberately obscured for decades. They represented the ideals of martial masculinity of the Old Japan;

they returned to a New Japan in which those ideals had not been wholly disavowed but were at the very least antiquated, regressive, and even embarrassing (if *bushidō*—the way of the warrior—had any relevance anymore, it was for the white-collar corporate salarymen who were engineering Japan's spectacular economic growth). Those ideals had been used as propaganda to mobilize the entire population for a disastrous war that cost millions of lives in Japan and elsewhere. If some admired the three holdouts for their resilience, others viewed them with pity, as "farcical" figures and victims of fascist indoctrination who had wasted three decades of their lives in a discredited, quixotic crusade (Igarashi 2016, 170–1; Trefalt 2003, 12, 45, 105). In that sense, it fed the prevailing narrative that the Japanese had been victims of the Asia-Pacific War rather than its perpetrators (Igarashi 2000, 37, 205; Trefalt 2003, 9, 109 159).

* * *

Onoda arrived in Lubang with orders to destroy an airfield and a pier of potential utility to the Allies. He had just left an audience in Manila with the Chief of Staff of the Fourteenth Area Army, Lt. General Mutō Akira (1892–1948). "You are absolutely forbidden to die by your own hand," Mutō reiterated. "It may take three years, it may take five, but whatever happens, we'll come back for you. Until then, so long as you have one soldier, you are to continue to lead him. You may have to live on coconuts. If that's the case, live on coconuts! Under no circumstances, are you [to] give up your life voluntarily" (Onoda 1974, 44).[3]

When Onoda landed on Lubang, he was given some fifty soldiers from different units, over whom he had no real authority, to do his work. No one had any idea what guerrilla warfare was, let alone the preparation or inclination to conduct it. "They all talked big about committing suicide and giving up their lives for the emperor," he recalled. "I had to listen to these men babbling at the mouth about dying for the cause," whereas "I could not even hint to anyone that I had orders not to die" (Onoda 1974, 44–5, 57–8).

After Allied troops arrived in western Lubang on February 28, 1945, Onoda and his ragtag team went into hiding. Having destroyed neither the airfield nor the pier, "I had disgraced myself as a secret warfare agent." To redeem himself, he planned a "desperate night attack" to "slaughter as many Americans as I could," but by September, Onoda, Shimada, Akatsu, and Kozuka were just malnourished "stragglers from a defeated army" left on the island (Onoda 1974, 68, 88).

In September 1949, Akatsu made a fourth and final attempt to desert and surrender. The man whom Onoda considered a "weakling" survived alone and surrendered in the eastern village of Looc in June 1950. Later that year, the remaining three discovered a letter in Akatsu's hand, saying, "When I surrendered the Philippine troops greeted me as a friend." They later spied Akatsu in a search party dispatched to find them. Unpersuaded by the deserter's note, Onoda also thought other leaflets and loudspeaker announcements were rendered in "strange-sounding Japanese," translations in which the "choice of words sounded American" (*eigoppoi* Japanese, which even if grammatically correct and intelligible is not idiomatically proper). If the language sounded odd or if someone unexpected, like a neighbor, appeared in a picture of their families, the three holdouts convinced themselves that something was fishy (Onoda 1974, 76–7, 92–3, 111).

In June 1953, Shimada was seriously wounded with a bullet through the knee in a firefight with a local fisherman. Onoda, who was hit in his right-hand ring finger, nursed him back to health, but on May 7, 1954, Shimada was shot again, through the forehead, by a Philippine soldier training for counterinsurgency warfare against the communist Hukbalahap rebels ("Huks"). Onoda and Kozuka swore revenge. Shortly thereafter, they managed to evade another search party, which they later learned had included Onoda's brother Toshirō and Kozuka's brother Fukuji (Onoda 1974, 101–8, 117–18). It may not have mattered, for Onoda Hiroo had vowed not to surrender until his direct commander, Major Taniguchi Yoshimi (1911–??), ordered him to do so.[4]

Onoda and Kozuka literally soldiered on, firm in the belief that the IJA would "send a landing force to Lubang, or at least … send secret agents to establish contact with us." The regime had taught them to expect the war to last a hundred years, so for nineteen years after Shimada's death, they prepared for this anticipated operation. They mapped the entire island and conducted "beacon-fire raids," burning bails of rice harvested by local farmers to signal to their comrades; they captured and interrogated islanders about what was going on; they fired on police and evaded search parties. They also murdered and robbed people. Locals called them "mountain devils."

In 1965, they stole a transistor radio and always voraciously read Japanese newspapers left for them. They learned about the 1964 Tokyo Olympics, the bullet train, the Vietnam War, and efforts to find them. Every year, they listened to the annual

New Year's Eve music program *Red and White Song Battle* (*Kōhaku uta gassen*) on the public broadcaster NHK. "[I]n a way," Onoda mused:

> the newspapers confirmed that the war was still going on, because they told a lot about life in Japan. If Japan had really lost the war, there should not be any life in Japan. Everybody should be dead. . . . I sincerely believed that Japan would not surrender so long as one Japanese remained alive. Conversely, if one Japanese were left alive, Japan could not have surrendered. (Onoda 1974, 109, 125, 155, 157–8, 160, 168)

On October 19, 1972, Kozuka was shot and killed in a skirmish with police and villagers. After angry islanders hacked Kozuka's corpse with machetes, the Japanese government dispatched a mission to retrieve it (the Philippine government gave him a funeral in Manila as a gesture of friendship) and find Onoda. He recognized the voices of his sister Chie and brother Tadao on loudspeakers, as well as Tadao's handwriting on a note. His father also came to Lubang and left a calligraphic haiku:

Not even an echo
Responds to my call in the
Summery mountains.

Yet Onoda remained convinced he was being tricked by American forces to give himself up (Onoda 1974, 174–82, 190). The harder people looked for him, he surmised, the more significant a military threat his mission must indeed be (see Figure 1.1).

Figure 1.1: *Suzuki Norio and Lt. Onoda Hiroo, Lubang Island, the Philippines, February 1974 (Wikipedia Commons).*

* * *

Upon hearing of Kozuka's death, college dropout and seasoned traveler Suzuki Norio (1949–86) decided to embark on a private mission to find Onoda, "a [wild] panda, and the Abominable Snowman [*yuki otoko*]" (Suzuki 1974; Echigoya 1992). After finding Suzuki's camp on February 20, 1974, it took some time to allay Onoda's suspicions that Suzuki was just another agent of the Americans sent to foil his mission. One reassuring clue was that, unlike the islanders, Suzuki wore wool socks with his rubber sandals (apparently, only a real Japanese would do that). Suzuki was likewise worried that if he returned with Taniguchi (then a bookseller in Miyazaki prefecture), Onoda would simply disappear again, but the soldier promised not to. He even allowed Suzuki to take a photograph of the two of them together so that others would believe his story (Onoda 1974, 196–206; Echigoya 1992, 87–8). Still, while he waited, Onoda came up with all kinds of explanations to justify his continued suspicions that Lubang was of such strategic importance that the Allies were desperate to remove him. He dug in, prepared to stay another twenty years if necessary (Onoda 1974, 207–9).

When Suzuki returned, he left two sets of orders for Onoda at a previously designated place: General Yamashita Tomoyuki's (1885–1946) original order for the Fourteenth Area Army to stand down, which Onoda had seen before on leaflets; and the other from the Special Squadron, which Taniguchi would present to him orally within the next few days. Onoda surrendered on March 9 and, despite being a "prisoner of war," received respectful salutes from Philippine troops (Onoda 1974, 217). His brother Toshirō met him in Lubang and accompanied him to Manila to turn over his sword and receive a formal pardon from President Ferdinand Marcos (who, with characteristic theatricality, insisted that Onoda appear in the tattered uniform he had worn and repeatedly patched). His war was finished.

* * *

After his repatriation in 1974, Onoda wasted little time writing a memoir; both Japanese and English versions were published later that same year. The memoir is an odd mix of critical reflection on his gullibility and ideological bullheadedness and an honorable warrior's self-exculpatory survival narrative. Beatrice Trefalt (2003) observes that Onoda was "very comfortable as a public figure, much more so than Yokoi. If the media manipulated Yokoi, Onoda manipulated the media, using it very much to his advantage, playing thoroughly the role of the tough, dedicated, rigid intelligence officer of the Nakano School, the 'paragon of military virtue' that seemed so fascinating to the Japan of the 1970s" (149). Yet what some admired as his devotion to duty, others considered slavish adherence to a fascist ideology that sanctioned violence in the emperor's name—Onoda himself said the monarch had made him a "slave" and should have abdicated to take responsibility for the war (Igarashi 2016, 180, 263n26).

In fact, historian Yoshikuni Igarashi (2016) bluntly notes, "Onoda and his men shot local people and took their food" (174) (by contrast, Nakamura fished and raised crops while Yokoi ate breadfruit, mice, snails, and toads). Journalist Fujinami Osamu (1977) later traveled to Lubang to interview people whose family members Onoda and Kozuka had brutally slain as they tended their crops. In these accounts, Hiroo was no hero but rather a "murderous straggler who had terrorized the locals," whom he derisively called *donkō*.[5] He seemed to expect a medal for not raping women or abducting children, even though he claimed (fallaciously) such acts "were within the range allowed by the international law of war" (Igarashi 2016, 153, 173–4, 187, 198, 200, 209). Lubang residents were thus the only people in Pacific Asia who continued to be tormented by Japanese troops after the war.

Expressing little remorse for robbing and killing his neighbors (he may well have stayed hidden to avoid prosecution), Onoda at least admitted his self-delusion: "I constructed an imaginary world that would fit in with the oath I had taken fifteen years earlier." Contrary to the popular media narrative that Onoda's group did not know the Second

World War had ended, they were told repeatedly via leaflets, family photographs, personalized entreaties, loudspeakers from aircraft, and search parties that included their own close relatives. "By that time, Kozuka and I had developed so many fixed ideas that we were unable to understand anything that did not conform with them" (Onoda 1974, 126–8). Crafting bizarre, convoluted alternative explanations for a truth they could not bear, they modified reality to suit their ideology.

Neither is it true that nobody knew the holdouts were there. Islanders, local police, and Philippine soldiers certainly did; the Japanese press reported nearly every sighting, and the Ministry of Health and Welfare sent search parties after almost each one. Their stubborn refusal to countenance news of defeat clearly was not typical of Japanese military personnel but did indicate the tenacity of fascist indoctrination in some individuals. Moreover, Onoda's intelligence training predisposed him not to underestimate the clever duplicity of the enemy, who cannily employed some of the same PSYOPS tactics that the IJA had.

It was precisely the lingering power of this indoctrination that Toshiko Akiyoshi found so tragic when she learned of Onoda's eventual surrender. "My heart ached for Lt. Onoda," she wrote in her autobiography, "who had lost his all-important twenties, not to mention his thirties and forties, too," vainly fighting a long-finished war. He represented an entire brainwashed generation that had wasted its youth in a horrendous, vainglorious, and self-destructive conflagration. Onoda would become her muse for "Kogun," the title track of the forthcoming debut album by the Toshiko Akiyoshi-Lew Tabackin Big Band (TA-LTBB) (she finished and recorded

"Kogun" within a month of his return and may not have known about his crimes against Lubang islanders, which the Ministry tried to hide). By incorporating musical elements and aural textures from Japanese *nō* theater (often anglicized "noh") and *gagaku* court music, Akiyoshi captured the woe of Onoda's story. She sympathized with him in part because "I thought I myself was also a lone soldier in America" (Akiyoshi 1996, 21, 212–13; Nishida 2019, 93).

What did she mean by this? In the liner notes to the Japanese release of *Kogun* she alluded to her triple-outsider status (Tabackin jokes that she's "demographically challenged"), a female Asian immigrant whose peers were overwhelmingly American-born males of African or European descent, who felt "pathetic and comical" performing the "culture of a different country" (*ikoku no bunka*). Akiyoshi no doubt identified on some level with a man the age of her older sisters, whose life was disrupted by war, relocation, culture shock, and varying degrees of privation, whose survival required discipline, perseverance, and grit, and who earned admiration from the unlikeliest of quarters.

2 The Long Yellow Road

I want to keep on creating sounds that will add something to the American tradition, without distorting its basic character.

TOSHIKO AKIYOSHI, QUOTED IN FEATHER (1978B)

The Cozy Quartet was not Japan's first bebop band, but it was the baddest.

For one thing, it had the enthusiastic endorsement of one Hampton Hawes (1928–77), an American soldier from Los Angeles who had played piano with Charlie Parker and Howard McGhee, recorded with Dexter Gordon and Shorty Rogers, and was a fixture at the Lighthouse jazz club in Hermosa Beach (Hawes 1979).

For another, the Cozy Quartet featured an alto saxophonist who really got Bird (Parker). The twenty-year-old Watanabe Sadao (b. 1933) didn't quite have his technique and sight-reading together yet, but he had the *feel*, a rare quality among wannabe beboppers.

This was no mean feat. By the early 1950s, Japanese musicians had been playing jazz for almost thirty years. But Parker himself asserted that bebop was "something entirely separate and apart" from earlier iterations of jazz.[1] It was a movement that emerged in New York in the early 1940s in response to multiple social, economic, cultural, and racial conditions (DeVeaux 1997). Musicians who played mainly in the big bands gathered for after-hours jam sessions at Minton's Playhouse in Harlem, creating a new music emphasizing virtuosic technique, harmonic density, rhythmic complexity, and spontaneous interplay, and which demanded attentive listening as opposed to dancing. A quintessential modernist art, bebop spotlighted the individual improviser's voice and upset prevailing canons of aesthetic value that marked jazz as popular culture—the "other" of capital-A Art—and its practitioners as entertainers rather than artists.

Bebop came to Japan as a purely musical challenge with little to no social context. Even for experienced Japanese musicians, this puzzling, labyrinthine new style was a lot to take in, both musically and conceptually. And if they were hired to play at clubs frequented by African American servicemen during the Allied Occupation (1945–52), they'd be asked to play it—well.

Two groups, Clambake 9 and Gramercy 6, took respectable stabs at it. But the Cozy Quartet had it down. True, the bassist couldn't improvise his bass lines at 250–300 beats per minute like Oscar Pettiford or Curley Russell; the bandleader had to transcribe them from American recordings for him to read onstage. But when some cocksure American GI with a horn showed up wanting to sit in, the bandleader would call a tune like "Fine and Dandy" or "Get Happy" at a blistering tempo. Often those guys left the stage with their horns between their legs (Akiyoshi 1996, 104; "Toshiko Akiyoshi" 1998).

Another reason the Cozy Quartet was so bad was that its members refused to play dance tunes or vocal numbers.

They were too cool for that. It was all bebop, all the time. Consequently, they lost many gigs or didn't score them in the first place.

Finally, the CQ was probably the only major jazz band in the country whose bandleader wore a skirt and heels. But she was definitely one of the cats. She spent her days in Yokohama and Tokyo jazz coffeeshops (*jazu kissa*), furiously transcribing "heads" (melodies) of tunes, solos, and those bass lines. She was mad about Bud Powell and befriended Hawes in part because they both revered him. She had played in dance bands and well-known combos such as the Ichiban Octet, Gay Stars, and Six Lemons for years but was done with all that. She had no idea what the future held for her, but she was only going to play music on her own terms, much to the annoyance of some club owners and audiences.

On March 18, 1956, not long after arriving in the United States with a scholarship to Boston's Berklee School of Music, she appeared on the popular television quiz show *What's My Line?* Celebrity panelists asked her a series of questions to guess her profession, which was "jazz pianist." She sat next to host Franklin Heller, wearing a kimono and smiling shyly, her voice barely audible.[2] American audiences found her adorable. Club owners, bandsmen, and presumptuous yet untalented GI musicians back in Japan would not have recognized the tough, single-minded woman whom they could neither manipulate nor deter. But it was indeed she, and even when she performed occasionally in kimono, American jazz musicians soon learned to take her as seriously as she took her art.

To this day, Toshiko Akiyoshi uses the word "bebop" in her email address.

* * *

"Long Yellow Road" ("Kiiroi nagai michi"), first recorded for the 1961 *Toshiko Akiyoshi Recital* trio album, has become her theme song and musical memoir. Its title refers to the long roads and endless horizons of Manchuria, where she was born; to her "yellow" race; and to the journey that brought her to the United States, where she would apprentice and mingle with the canonical figures of modern jazz—and become one herself (Honda 1984, 39–40). With each step of her career and each new achievement and accolade, the long yellow road lengthens and carries her on an "endless journey" (Akiyoshi 2017). At this writing, she is ninety-four years old and still performing around the world solo and with small groups, oftentimes with her husband, Lew Tabackin, whose faith in her talents urged her on. That long yellow road had many twists, turns, potholes, pitstops, and barriers.

Toshiko Akiyoshi was born to Japanese settler parents in Manchuria, a contested terrain in East Asian history and historiography.[3] It was the homeland of China's last imperial dynasty, the Qing (1644–1911), but many others made claims to it: Chinese called it their "northeast" (indeed, despite Manchu prohibitions, by the dynasty's end, well over 80 percent of the population were Han Chinese); historian Sin Ch'ae-ho (1880–1936) claimed it had once been Korean territory; Russians wanted to build a trans-Siberian railroad through Manchuria for access to China and the Pacific; and Japanese called it their economic "lifeline" (*seimeisen*) to natural resources.

Akiyoshi's birth on December 12, 1929, in the ancient city of Liaoyang, occurred during an interregnum between major military interventions to secure Japanese control of Manchuria: the assassination of uncooperative local warlord Zhang Zuolin (1875–1928); and a full-scale military intervention in September 1931. The following year, the League of Nations rejected Japanese claims that "Manchukuo" was a fully sovereign nation-state led by China's last Manchu emperor. Although her family flourished, Akiyoshi grew up in a precarious environment, under the protection of Japan's Kwantung Army while surrounded by resentful, sometimes hostile locals.

Her father, Katsurō (1891–1953), went to Harbin immediately after the First World War as an employee of the Suzuki Trading Company, one of Japan's largest and most prominent corporations. As expressed most obnoxiously in the Twenty-One Demands of 1915, Japanese businesses had major economic ambitions in China. However, the postwar recession and catastrophic 1923 Kantō Earthquake scuttled Suzuki's prospects in China. Katsurō stayed in Manchuria with his growing family, working for Fuji Spinning in Liaoyang and later opening his own trading company. Between 1921 and 1929, he and his wife Shigeko (1896–1988) had four daughters, Hisako, Miyoko, Reiko, and Toshiko.

In the 1930s, Shigeko relocated to Dalian so that the girls could attend Japanese middle and high schools. Though they comprised a privileged class in Manchuria's multiethnic society, Japanese students were nonetheless required to learn Mandarin from third grade. Toshiko recalled in 2008, "if I stayed in China for, maybe, one month, without talking Japanese . . . I think I'd get [it] back."

Compared to the economic misery so many Japanese endured during the 1930s, both at home and in agrarian settlements in Manchuria, the Akiyoshis prospered in a "rich cultural environment." Hisako studied traditional dance (*buyō*), and Katsurō was a *nō* (Japanese theater) enthusiast who studied the *kotsuzumi*, a small hourglass hand drum, the pitch of which can be altered by squeezing and releasing tension cords connecting the drumheads. Her childhood familiarity with *nō* had a major impact on Toshiko's music, as she used *tsuzumi* drums and *kakegoe* (drum calls) in "Kogun" and *Minamata*.

The Akiyoshis also had an organ in the home, on which Toshiko learned to plunk out "La Cucaracha" and sections of *La Traviata*. When she was in first grade, she heard a third-grader play the third movement ("Alla Turca") of Mozart's Piano Sonata No. 11 and requested piano lessons. Liaoyang had no specialized piano instructors, so her school's music teacher taught her twice a week after school. Even the harsh Manchurian winters did not discourage her from attending. In high school, her teacher was Yang Xiaoyi, a Chinese man who had studied at Tokyo's Musashino Academia Musicae and spoke Japanese well.[4]

The Akiyoshis were fairly insulated from the war (officially labeled an "incident," *jihen*) that broke out between Japan and Republican China in July 1937. Military operations in Manchuria focused primarily on the suppression of "bandits," an epithet that lumped together actual gangs of thieves and guerrilla resistance fighters who sabotaged infrastructure and terrorized Japanese settlers. After the attack on Pearl Harbor, expectations for more active civilian participation rose. Young Toshiko and her classmates wore military-style uniforms and trained with wooden swords and *naginata* (halberds). Since "luxury" was branded "the enemy" (*zeitaku wa teki da!*), people who played piano were often castigated for their "bourgeois bearing" (*burujowa tekina taido*) during a "time of emergency" (*hijōji*). Nevertheless, she persisted.

In year four of high school, telling each parent that the other had approved, Toshiko volunteered to be a military nurse. She observed seasoned nurses caring for wounded soldiers, but the war ended before she could do the work herself. Like other Japanese settlers in Manchukuo, China, Taiwan, and Korea, the Akiyoshis were spared the air raids and extreme privation afflicting the Japanese metropole. But what happened to them was bad enough. Soviet troops—notorious for savage sexual violence, looting, and wanton murder as they overran Nazi- and Japanese-occupied territories—ransacked their house, distributing their belongings to Chinese waiting outside to sell them all. Toshiko recalled cutting her hair short to disguise herself as a boy.

About a year of repeated Soviet and Chinese Communist intrusions passed before the family could return to their hometown, Beppu, on Kyūshū island. Like other repatriates (*hikiagesha*), they had lost everything they could not carry onto the ship and were grudgingly received back in their devastated homeland, where food, housing, and jobs were already scarce. *Hikiagesha* were typically stigmatized and alienated, "rejected . . . as insufficiently Japanese," potentially diseased, and living reminders of Japan's collapsed empire. Compared to the suffering of people in Japan, theirs was minimized in remembrance of the war. But as Lori Watt (2009) contends, "this alienation contributed to the making of some of Japan's most insightful critics," among whom she mentions Toshiko Akiyoshi (10, 13).

Unable to finish high school (her class were "honorary graduates"), sixteen-year-old Toshiko found a way to support her family while getting her eager fingers back onto a piano. Commercial dancehalls, which the Home Ministry had shut down in 1940, were sprouting up everywhere: some were for US troops (segregated by rank and race) and others for Japanese—never the twain were to meet. However, the Americans could not jitterbug without Japanese musical labor. Toshiko played in both settings, learning American popular songs on the fly from stock arrangements. For a while, she also performed as a singing accordionist.

Despite his family's economic travails, Katsurō was furious that Toshiko worked in a dancehall; only "bad girls" (*furyō shōjo*) worked there. Her parents had hoped she would go to medical school. But she enjoyed the work, which was relatively easy and lucrative, and spent her afternoons practicing piano before each evening's performance.

Impressed by her playing, a Mr. Fukui invited her to his home to listen to the record that changed her life, Teddy Wilson's rendition of "Sweet Lorraine."[5] In contrast to the "barbarous" (*yabanteki*) music she played in the dance hall, she was struck by Wilson's "clean" technique, which sounded like a "string of pearls." Toshiko thought, "I want to play like that!"

In 1947, at age seventeen, Toshiko moved to Fukuoka, Kyūshū's largest city, to take the piano chair in Yamada Ryūtarō's orchestra, the house band in a US military officers' club. She spent her afternoons there listening to American jazz records and eventually began transcribing both composed and improvised parts, a practice for which she would become famous. In the summer of 1948, Akiyoshi left for Tokyo with Yamada's blessing. Over the next two years, she played in a show band, the Blue Coats, Ichiban Octet, Gay Stars, and Six Lemons, in concert venues and US military clubs. She bought her first piano, on which she received an all-night master class from Jeff Clarkson, pianist for Les Brown's Band of Renown, during its USO-sponsored visit to Tokyo. She befriended and studied with GI jazzmen Hampton Hawes and Norbert "Bert" de Coteaux (who became a successful producer, arranger, and songwriter in the 1960s–1970s).[6] In 1951, she met and jammed with members of bass legend Oscar Pettiford's band, including trombonist J.J. Johnson, during its USO-sponsored visit.

Akiyoshi was more than content to freelance as "the highest-paid" side player in Tokyo and Yokohama. However, after hearing Bud Powell's recording of "Body and Soul" on the US Armed Forces Radio Service ("He was the one who *really* hit my heart"), she musically outgrew most of her employers.[7] Akiyoshi was among a small coterie of musicians who tired of playing for dancers and voraciously absorbed the breakneck tempos, thick harmonies, and sinuous melodies of bebop. She spent hours at Yokohama's Chigusa *jazu kissa*, furiously transcribing Powell's recordings; proprietor Yoshida Mamoru (1913–94) patiently replayed records several times to help her get it all down accurately. By 1953, she had founded the Cozy Quartet and, along with fellow Powell aficionado Moriyasu Shōtarō (1924–55), had become the undisputed leader of Japan's bebop scene (Atkins 2001, 196–209).

Her story thereafter is well known among jazz cognoscenti. When Norman Granz's Jazz at the Philharmonic package tour came to Japan in November 1953, Canadian pianist Oscar Peterson caught the Cozy Quartet at Ginza's Tennessee club and urged Granz to record her. "I usually listen to a player before I record," Granz told her, "but Oscar said that I don't have to listen to you." In two all-night sessions with Peterson's rhythm section (J. C. Heard, Ray Brown, and Herb Ellis), Akiyoshi recorded the 10-inch album *Toshiko's Piano*.

"Actually, after that, my life was the same as before: I was still barely paying the rent," she laughingly recalled. "I had high respect from people, but that doesn't mean I had a lot of work. I never had commercial success because I never played commercial music." But the notice *Toshiko's Piano* received—including a three-star review in *Down Beat*—gave her ambition to go to the United States. "Jazz is a social art: if you are surrounded by better players, you become better at it." She was "the biggest frog in a small pond" and could only improve by playing with her heroes.

The most feasible way to go was on a student visa. Boston's Berklee School of Music offered her a full scholarship; the novelty of a Japanese "girl" playing jazz was a good way "to advertise the school," she later said. Arriving in January 1956, Akiyoshi immediately immersed herself in top-flight jazz circles. She felt obligated to finish her schooling because of the scholarship (and did so in three and a half years), but she spent as much time as she could in the thriving jazz clubs of Boston, New York, and Philadelphia. Miles Davis, Count Basie, Max Roach, Bud Powell, and many others welcomed her warmly. Berklee allowed her to lead bands at venues like the Hickory House and Newport Jazz Festival, and to record under her own name for Storyville and Verve, but not to join other artists' groups. "I didn't want to be a leader and somehow, I was pushed into [being] a leader... . I would be the happiest person if I were a great sideman, side player." Most significantly, she earned the esteem of her greatest hero. "You're the best female piano player," Powell told her. "He said that to me, and that would carry me for a *long* time; when I had a hard time, almost quit, I'd say, 'Well, Bud Powell said that, so I must have something'" (see Figure 2.1).

Akiyoshi graduated from Berklee with thorough training in Joseph Schillinger's (1895–1943) mathematically based

Figure 2.1: *Toshiko Akiyoshi at home before taking the stage at her first appearance at the Newport Jazz Festival, November 11, 1956. Photo by Ben Martin/Getty Images.*

Method of Music Composition and a husband, alto saxophonist Charlie Mariano, a veteran of Stan Kenton and Shelly Manne's groups. Along with Yusef Lateef and Don Cherry, in the 1960s Mariano would become a pioneer in so-called "world music," learning the *nādhasvaram*, a South Indian double-reed instrument, and recording two albums with Akiyoshi's former sideman, Watanabe Sadao. Through the early 1960s, they co-led a quartet with drummer Eddie Marshall and bassist Gene Cherico.

Akiyoshi's reputation was such that Charles Mingus invited her to join his group. She was stunned, but he said, "It's true that there are a lot of good players, but you're a new name . . . and a new name is very important to the group." "Now, that really impressed me," she said, "because Mingus, he could've said to me, 'It's good for you, you'll get recognition,' which I *did*. . . . He could've said that to me, but he didn't." Mingus was notoriously abusive, and she heard other musicians mutter, "How is he gonna hit *her*?" (Santoro 2000, 248). However, she remembered Mingus affectionately as being unfailingly supportive of her aspirations as a composer. She appreciated how he ran rehearsals in his apartment: "He didn't have any music: he sang, and we all had to learn that. I think that's the best way." "Mingus used to repeat a melody numerous times. I used to dream about his melodies when I went to sleep."

Alternating with Jaki Byard, Akiyoshi played piano for Mingus at the Five Spot for the latter half of 1962 (switching to bass when he took over the piano on "Eat That Chicken") and at his chaotic Town Hall concert on October 12. According to trombonist Jimmy Knepper, she was a reluctant participant in the call-and-response part of "Fables of Faubus": when

Mingus hollered, "Name me someone who's ridiculous," in apparent frustration, Akiyoshi stood up and yelled back, "*You're* ridiculous. *I'm* ridiculous. We're *all* ridiculous!" (Priestly 1982, 134–6).

In early 1963, Akiyoshi returned to Japan with Mariano, to be with her mother when giving birth to their daughter, Monday Michiru (born August 19); they also hoped to enliven Tokyo's moribund jazz scene. They left Japan in February 1965, completely dispirited by the "absenteeism and general apathy" of their workshop band (Atkins 2001, 212–13). They clearly believed the Japanese were good enough brass and wind players but deficient rhythmically. On the 1964 album *Toshiko Mariano and Her Big Band*, the first to feature her orchestrations, the rhythm section consisted of Akiyoshi and two American ringers, drummer Jimmy Cobb and bassist Paul Chambers.

Not long after they returned to the United States, the couple separated. Mariano wanted Akiyoshi to care for his four children from a previous marriage, as well as Michiru, which would have essentially suspended her own career. They divorced in 1967. Akiyoshi did not lack for gigs (she rejoined Mingus' group in 1966), but they barely covered her rent. Unable to tour, hire overnight babysitters, or afford a live-in caregiver, she sent her daughter to live with her sister Miyoko in Beppu until she could build a more solid economic foundation. "I think my daughter had a very, very difficult childhood."

Determining that she could make more of a mark as a composer than as a player, Akiyoshi prepared a recital for October 7, 1967, at Town Hall, the same venue where Mingus had premiered his *Epitaph*.[8] She raised money by teaching at a college jazz clinic and playing in Holiday Inn cocktail lounges throughout the United States. In addition to solo and trio performances, she prepared full orchestrations of five original Japan-themed compositions, including "The Village," "Let's Roll in Sake," "Sumi-e," and "Henpecked Old Man." After she had booked the venue, Mayor John Lindsay declared October 7 Jazz Day in New York City, so there were competing black-tie events throughout the city that suppressed turnout for her concert. But Mingus was there, toting a camera, and she got a favorable review in the *New York Times*. "But . . . it didn't do anything! It didn't do any good," she chuckled. "After that I was *still* barely paying the rent!"

It did *some* good, however. While looking for a tenor saxophonist for her recital, Akiyoshi subbed in Clark Terry's big band at the Half Note.

> If you know the Half Note, the middle was the bar, a circular bar, and the band was upstairs. Now, the room was . . . divided in two, one side and another side. Then when the big band went on the top, the rhythm section was on this side, the horn players were kind of spread, so to speak. So, I was there, and Clark started with a D-flat blues or something like that. . . . I heard a tenor player play, and it was, boy, that like knocked me out! It was an interesting combination . . . it had Lucky Thompson's family tree, which was very rare to hear in those days—I guess it still is today. But what he played was like a semi-cross between Coltrane and Sonny Rollins. (Akiyoshi 2008)

Love at first sound? Perhaps (she also wondered, "Who is this guy, he can't be any good, I never heard of him") (Harrington 1980). In any case, it initiated a musical and personal partnership that has endured for over half a century, rooted in genuine mutual admiration for each other's artistry. "Meeting a good partner is important," Akiyoshi remarked. "After all, Ellington had Strayhorn" (Rothbart 1980, 15).

* * *

Very few American cities have populated the jazz pantheon as prodigiously as Philadelphia has. John Coltrane, Jimmy Smith, Lee Morgan, Philly Joe Jones, the Heath and Brecker Brothers, Ray Bryant, Beryl Booker, McCoy Tyner, Pat Martino, Joe Chambers, Archie Shepp, Alphonso Johnson, Byard Lancaster, Joey DeFrancesco, Hasaan Ibn Ali, Jamaaladeen Tacuma, Christian McBride, and Odean Pope are but a few. Lewis Barry Tabackin (b. March 26, 1940) belongs in such an exalted company.

Raised in ethnically diverse, working-class South Philly, Tabackin discovered jazz at age four when his mother took him to a movie theater that had a house band and occasionally featured stars like Cab Calloway and Lionel Hampton. "They did a certain effect with lighting, where it seemed like the room was rocking and shaking. I think that had an impact that eventually led to my interest in jazz" ("#13 Toshiko Akiyoshi" 2012; "Lew Tabackin Biography"). Initially interested in clarinet, he was assigned a flute at age thirteen and picked up tenor at age fifteen after hearing an Al Cohn record at a neighbor's house. "I had a sound in my head, and I knew exactly what I wanted," he recalled. "Many don't find their sound because they don't know what they want, and they try to sound like others. Shortly afterwards, I went to jam sessions." "They were fairly tolerant of novices" (Perez 2016; AAJ Staff 2003a).

Unlike most saxophonists who double on flute, Tabackin started on that instrument, earning a degree in flute performance from the Philadelphia Conservatory of Music in 1962. He readily concurs with the critical consensus that he has distinct identities on each instrument (highlighted on his 1978 LP, *Dual Nature*). However, his tenor saxophone alone has multiple personalities, sometimes evoking the full, tender sound of Swing-Era giants like Coleman Hawkins, Lester Young, Ben Webster, and Don Byas, and at others a tougher, throatier tone that nimbly navigates knotty harmonic progressions with lyricism, control, and a strong sense of coherence. "Instead of emulating and copying their notes I try to absorb certain abstract qualities—an aura, or essence that I hear, which to me is the essential spirit of the music, and it becomes part of my musical expression" (Tabackin 2000, 4). Like Sonny Rollins, he is famous for virtuosic cadenzas. If the aesthetic ideal in jazz is simultaneously to nod reverentially to tradition while moving aggressively into uncharted space with fearless abandon, then Lew Tabackin—who has been called the "last of the big-toned tenors" (Harris 2016)—exemplifies this as well as anyone. "To respect tradition is very important," Akiyoshi has said. "But Lew's greatness is that he always puts something of his own on the top" ("#13 Toshiko Akiyoshi" 2012).

After graduating from the conservatory, like many musicians of his generation, Tabackin served in the US Army for several years, then dove right into the deep end of the jazz pool, New York City, joining Calloway and Terry's respective bands. When Akiyoshi heard him at the Half Note (he had seen her play with Mingus at Pep's Musical Bar in Philly before he joined the Army), she asked him to play at her Town Hall recital. He agreed, but then wound up joining the Jones-Lewis orchestra for a more lucrative three-week tour. Though Tabackin jokes that this is still a sore subject in the household, Akiyoshi acknowledged, "For him, like any New York musician, they have to make a living.... If you have a two-week job instead of one, you take the two-week job. That is the way it goes" (AAJ Staff 2003b). He later joined Akiyoshi's combo for a gig in Hartford, CT, and appeared on the 1968 live album *Toshiko at Top of the Gate*.

In Hartford, "I took out my flute and I kind of grossed Toshiko out, because she hated all these saxophone players who played lousy flute. And she was like, 'Wow, he actually can play!'" (Tabackin 2023). Eventually, she composed pieces specifically to feature it. At the time, the Boehm System transverse flute was still a novelty instrument in jazz. Sam Most, Herbie Mann, Bobbi Humphrey, and Hubert Laws were among a small handful of specialists who made it a credible bebop instrument; saxophonists Frank Wess, James Moody, Eric Dolphy, Rahsaan Roland Kirk, Sam Rivers, and Yusef Lateef, among others, took up flute as a secondary instrument. But Tabackin does not consider himself to be a "bebop flutist," drawing his concept instead from other sources.

In 1969, the couple married. Their union was fortuitous and timely, and it resulted in some of the most exciting music of the late twentieth century. In creating her own voice by drawing on her "heritage" and thereby transforming a presumed liability into an asset, Toshiko Akiyoshi not only drew from the musical textures of *nō* and *gagaku* but also crafted her sonic signature around her husband's flute sound. Recognizing his versatility and singular ability to mimic on the metallic instrument both the end-blown *shakuhachi* and the transverse *nōkan* (both bamboo instruments), she composed pieces specifically for him.

Thus did an Asian immigrant and a Jewish American go beyond the conventions of big-band jazz by incorporating musical elements from outside the African and European diasporas, creating a sound and body of work marked by a "crosscultural sensibility that speaks less to a purity of form or idiomatic consistency than to a hybridized coherency" (Fellezs 2010, 55). Among their other accomplishments, they helped make the "quintessentially American" art form more cosmopolitan.

3 The Band

Having a big band is no picnic.
TOSHIKO AKIYOSHI (STEWART 1994)

Dig this: neither Toshiko Akiyoshi nor Lew Tabackin likes big bands.

Jazz orchestras are certainly exhausting and expensive to maintain. Eight weeks of work per year—usually including costly annual trips to Japan—was insufficient for keeping the orchestra solvent, so she and Tabackin supported theirs with solo work and commissions (Stewart 1994). They felt responsible for providing steady work yet "exhibited no ill feelings" when members had to take other, more lucrative jobs. Bandsmen sometimes expected higher pay because of the music's difficulty and the requirement that reedists play multiple instruments (Fellezs 2010, 50, 51).

Logistical and financial challenges aside, though, both have artistic reasons for their general aversion to big bands. Akiyoshi has said that, with the notable exception of Duke Ellington's orchestra, "Most big bands do not make my heart beat faster. Someone like Tommy Dorsey, one of those yesteryear bands that people think of when they think of jazz big bands, I'm not very fond of." "Basie had a great band," she conceded. "Everybody swings together; they did it better than anybody. But it still does not make my heart beat faster" (Stewart 1994).

Although a veteran of some of modern jazz's most prestigious orchestras, Tabackin's opinion is more commonplace among musicians that big bands suppress the personal expression at the music's core. "[I]n an idiom in which the performer's role not only as interpreter but also as improviser remains central," Alex Stewart (2007) observes, there is a fundamental tension between the goals of the composer/arranger and those of the player (9–12, 310).

There is also a racial dimension to this: "One of the main criticisms leveled at big bands has been that they betray ideals of individualism in jazz and in African American culture," Stewart writes. For Black musicians, "jazz became an important site for construction of black masculinity that offered the possibility of undermining and subverting prevailing stereotypes rooted in minstrelsy and mass-mediated entertainment" (12–13, 310). "Before I came to New York," Tabackin told *Down Beat*, "I never played in any big bands and had no desire to play in them. I came from a small group background. And when I came to New York, all of a sudden—especially since I'm a white player—I found myself in big bands, although I couldn't even read a chart" (Feather 1976, 16). "If you're a jazz player, you want to play [improvise]," he adds. "The mythology was, if you were a white guy, you could read, if you were a black guy, you could play jazz" (Tabackin 2023). Although they made many small-group recordings with African American musicians, Akiyoshi and Tabackin always had trouble recruiting them for their orchestra (Stowe 2006, 293; Stewart 2007, 49, 55).

The decision to convene a rehearsal band after they relocated to Southern California in 1972, then, came not from any particular affinity for that format, but rather from Akiyoshi's desire to explore sounds, moods, colors, textures, and themes she could not create on piano alone, and Tabackin's enthusiasm for her compositions and the arrangements she had written for her 1967 Town Hall recital. Both required a full orchestra.

* * *

By the early 1970s, big bands appealed mainly to audiences who had grown up on them in the 1930s–1940s' Swing Era. Repertory bands with guaranteed nostalgia value—the ones Akiyoshi called "yesteryear bands"—led by Benny Goodman, Count Basie, Lionel Hampton, Woody Herman, Stan Kenton, and the ghosts of Tommy Dorsey and Glenn Miller—dominated this largely generational market. Until his death in 1974, Duke Ellington continued writing and recording extended thematic works such as the Grammy-winning *New Orleans Suite* (1970), but in concert he usually played familiar classics. Jazz critic Gunther Schuller wrote that after 1960, "jazz orchestral styles atrophied" and "very little of truly innovative achievement in arranging concepts can be claimed" (quoted in Stewart 2007, 7).

Of course, there were jazz orchestras writing and recording new material throughout the 1970s. The most prominent was that co-led by trumpeter Thad Jones and drummer Mel Lewis from 1965 to 1978, a racially integrated unit with a standing Monday night gig at New York's Village Vanguard and a book that mixed standards with Jones' original compositions. Buddy Rich, Louie Bellson, Maynard Ferguson, Gil Evans, Tito Puente, Bill Watrous, Eddie Palmieri, Bill Holman, Don Ellis, Ed Shaughnessy, Carla Bley and Michael Mantler (Jazz Composers Orchestra), and Sun Ra all led large ensembles; some of them reconfigured the standard format (five woodwinds, four trombones, four trumpets, and rhythm) and incorporated electric instruments and additional percussion.

Nonetheless, in the 1970s, the big band was generally "seen as an anachronism" and marginalized, discursively and physically, from the jazz mainstream: "big band music has its own category," Stewart (2007) remarks, "separate from jazz, in the statistics collected by the record industry (RIAA) and [as] reflected in the layout of the bins in many record stores. A customer looking for a Count Basie or Duke Ellington CD may not find it in the jazz section" (4). Shoppers hunting for Tommy Dorsey's records wouldn't have to flip through Eric Dolphy's to find them.

Jazz of the 1970s has generally been treated dismissively as the artistic nadir in the account of jazz history crafted by the 1980s' neo-conservative movement led by critic Stanley Crouch and trumpeter Wynton Marsalis, which provided the narrative theme for Ken Burns' 2000 documentary *Jazz*. Marsalis and Crouch's vitriol against Miles Davis for "selling out" with electric instruments and funk rhythms, and toward avant-gardists for improvising without harmonic structures and failing to "swing," mirrored the Reagan-era backlash against the countercultural "excesses" of the previous two decades. However sincere their harsh opinions and narrow conceptions of the jazz idiom, it was also shrewd marketing to validate their own revivalist agenda by denigrating an entire decade of musicking.

Crouch alleged that the core values of the art were under assault from undisciplined hacks. In op-eds, reviews, liner notes, pugnacious literary duels with other writers, and even a "sermon" written for Marsalis' 1989 LP *The Majesty of the Blues*,

Crouch contended that his protégé and other "Young Lions" were revolting "against the commercial dictates of fusion that threatened jazz during the '70s." Exhibiting "the true nature of aesthetic courage," they "rebelled by continuing to swing," while their elders rocked and funked all the way to the bank. "Ignoring the challenges of the fundamentals of an art form is less about courage than it is evasion," Crouch (2000) declared. "It is always easier not to swing than to swing, and when swing becomes a target for contempt, swinging becomes more important than ever."

Leaving aside the issue of whether fusion was indeed a middle finger aimed at "swing," by reductively claiming that nothing else was going on in the 1970s, Crouch and company disregarded too much jazz that swung aplenty. Though the "reactionary, even puritanical, forces" of fin-de-siècle neoclassicism had "largely overwritten with a single numbing word—*fusion*" the "rich legacy" of the 1970s (Shoemaker 2018, 1), jazz scholars are now exploring other aspects: "the political, self-help, and pedagogical projects of African American and multiracial jazz collectives"; the increasing prominence of female performers and composers; New York's "loft jazz" scene; the growth of academic jazz education; and the "proliferation of independent record companies" (Porter 2010). Still, this new work has paid little attention to the Toshiko Akiyoshi-Lew Tabackin Big Band (Shoemaker's book on 1970s jazz mentions it exactly once), an error this little book seeks to correct.

* * *

On August 18 and 19, 1970, Akiyoshi, Tabackin, bassist Bob Daugherty, and drummer Mickey Roker performed at the Japan World Exposition in Ōsaka. But by the time they moved to North Hollywood in July 1972, Akiyoshi had given up. "I felt as insignificant as the sand on the beach" (Swan 1980). "I didn't really make any impact, you know. I tried hard, I had my concert, got a good review and everything, but it didn't really change my life" (Akiyoshi 2008). Deciding that "the world doesn't need another piano player," she burned all her PR and other materials, set up their new home, and chauffeured her daughter to school and her husband to work.

Pianist John Lewis, leader of the famed Modern Jazz Quartet, had other plans for her. As music director for the 16th Annual Monterey Jazz Festival (September 21–23, 1973), he invited Akiyoshi to join him, Billy Taylor, and Ellis Larkins for the opening night's "Piano Playhouse" set. Although Lewis eventually became a close friend, at the time they only knew each other in passing, indicating that the invitation was based on her reputation as a player rather than on friendship. She claims it "saved my career" (Akiyoshi 2008).

Tabackin encouraged her to collect her five Town Hall recital charts and assembled a rehearsal band that convened from 10:15 a.m. to 1:00 p.m. on Wednesdays at the American Federation of Musicians Local 47 Union Hall in Burbank, where they could rent space for a nominal fifty cents. In the late 1960s and early 1970s, many in the entertainment industry relocated from New York to Los Angeles. Several jazz musicians joined this exodus, where they could "daylight" in movie and recording studios and enjoy warmer weather (Mercer 2004, 148; Hancock 2014, 158–9). Tabackin thus initially had little trouble finding musicians.

Only a few of the musicians were familiar with Akiyoshi's work. Aside from bassist Gene Cherico, with whom she played regularly in New York, trumpeters Mike Price and Bobby Shew both knew about her from playing in the Boston area. When he was studying composition at Berklee, Price (2023) recounts, the faculty were still talking about her and beaming over her success, years after she graduated. Shew purchased a book of her tunes published by Berklee (Akiyoshi 1960).

Inevitably, there was a winnowing process. "A lot of the guys couldn't relate to her music," Tabackin (2023) says. "They were used to going to a rehearsal band and being able to sightread everything. . . . And this was stuff that you had to concentrate on. And so, we'd weed out these people who couldn't deal with that and couldn't deal with a little woman standing in front of them telling them what to do." At the first rehearsal, Akiyoshi felt some skepticism, if not outright hostility, from some of the all-male, mostly white members. "I decided to say, 'Please' rather than 'I want . . .'" There was also "dissension" about who would play which parts, but "when the two-and-a-half-hour rehearsal ended, it was generally decided which players wanted to do it, which didn't, and which weren't capable" (Akiyoshi 1996, 207–8).

"She wrote very difficult stuff," the band's lead trumpeter, Bobby Shew, says, "and actually quite unlike anybody else had ever written for big band." He shared excerpts from manuscript books he kept to study and practice his parts (Figure 3.1).

> When I started . . . I kept saying, "God, Toshiko, you can't write like this. This is a trumpet." And she said, "Oh, please, Bobby, you try, please, Bobby, you try." And I thought, "Oh, she's so sweet."

Figure 3.1: Handwritten lead trumpet parts for "The Village," "Sumi-e," and "Henpecked Old Man." Courtesy of Bobby Shew.

> So I copied the difficult parts, and I took them home with me, and I got a chance to practice them until I set up all the neuromuscular patterns in my body, and I'd come back the next week and play, and she'd go [claps], "Wooo!" (Shew 2023)

Pointing at one of his handwritten scores, Shew noted the daunting intervallic leaps.

> It's really high. That's a concert A natural; it's a high B natural on the trumpet, just below double C. I mean, you're playing all this shit and all of a sudden, you've got to jump up there.... In the early days she was writing, she would do this on a piano, she would go [sings quick intervallic jump], "Oh, there's Bobby's part," you know [laughs]. A three-and-a-half-octave jump, you know... I was, "Holy crap," you know, this is not the kind of stuff that you do, normally do for a trumpet player. But I went to her one time and said, "Looks like Lew's flute part," and that's when [she said], "Bobby, please, you try."
>
> So I went home because I liked her, you know. I was thrilled to be trying to play something new; it was invigorating. This was a whole new thing. It was odd for us, and it was difficult, but it was like, "Wow!"... And I worked on that stuff until I could play it, and then she'd write higher, and I'd go, "Oh, Christ!"

Why put so much time and effort into a rehearsal band that might not go anywhere? "In the music business, for the most part, what you get paid for is garbage," Shew responds. "You're not really playing music, you're playing parts."

Still, "it was taxing." Shew once tried to hand off some of the lead parts to another trumpeter. "At the next rehearsal, she heard it, and she got pissed off. She said, 'You're the sound of the band, Bobby. Don't pass anything!'" But, he adds, "being on that band turned me into a better trumpet player than I think I would've ever become had I not been on that band. . . . It forced me to go home and create new ways to practice." Having never studied classical music, Shew picked up Théo Charlier's *36 Études Transcendantes pour Trompette* and "practiced the first three etudes up an octave . . . I gained control of the upper register by doing that."

Tabackin remembers that it was particularly challenging to find an appropriate drummer. Some had trouble following unusual song forms: for instance, "the number of bars was not symmetrical" on "Long Yellow Road," which consists of sections of eight, twenty, and eight measures. The music also required switching drumming styles. "The concept . . . was to be like a big band, but when somebody got to play a solo, it was a small band." Eminent jazz critic Leonard Feather (1914–94), who became one of their most ardent supporters and wrote *Kogun*'s sleeve notes for the American version, remarked on the drumming in his lukewarm review of the band's first live show on February 11, 1974, at Pasadena's Ice House (now a comedy club). The band "needed a more powerful drummer. Peter Donald failed to provide the necessary imagination and drive essential to a big band."[1]

Feather was rather pleased that Donald was touring with another group, and drum legend Shelly Manne filled in when the TA-LTBB played its first major concert at LA's Wilshire Ebell Theater on May 22, 1974. "Manne's guest membership in the band was tantamount to an insurance policy. It was a major plus to hear him, after all these years leading small combos, driving a big band as few drummers can."[2] "Shelly could read

ANYTHING," Shew says, "but he had a certain way of playing the ride cymbal that didn't always match the figures that Tosh wrote, much 'looser'!" Tabackin insists that Manne drummed marvelously, but he also praises Donald for hitting his stride at a seaside concert in Redondo Beach. "All of a sudden, all of the problems disappeared. It happened. I knew if he kept on doing it, [he'd figure it out]."

Feather had a few other criticisms in his review of the February Ice House show:

> Orchestrally, standard big band devices are employed, such as the sectional use of passages by four trumpets or five saxophones...
>
> Occasionally the palette was expanded through colorful voicings that recalled, at their best moments, the incandescence of a Gil Evans score. But there are few radical departures either in texture or structure...
>
> The band's weakness is a failure to frame more adequately its principal strength, namely Toshiko's mastery of the piano. There should be more orchestral numbers built around her along the lines of that darkly attractive 5/4 work, "The Village."

The band played the Los Angeles County Spring Jazz Festival (May 19) and four more shows at the Ice House (June 24, July 29, August 25, and December 1). Yet throughout the nine years of the LA-based incarnation of their orchestra, Akiyoshi and Tabackin did not try to keep it out on the road more than a few weeks a year. In 1980, *Down Beat* reported that touring was so expensive that "the best profits... were made by airline companies." The leaders paid them well, and weekly rehearsals continued, but the guys in the band also had other, steadier gigs. Beyond that, Akiyoshi admitted,

> my main responsibility is to create music. Lew and I decided we'd like to have a balance between the number of weeks we go out, and leave the rest as free time for myself, to keep creating and do some piano playing, which I've neglected in the past several years. This would also give Lew time to do his pianoless trio (Rothbart 1980, 15).

When they did perform, Akiyoshi was a dynamic, visually arresting conductor. Wearing long, elegant dresses (hippie-style ones in the 1970s) or sharp pantsuits, and sometimes sunglasses, she became something of a fashion icon. Working without a score, she made the music visible with her authoritative gestures and cues. "When conducting," Linda Dahl (1995) observed, "Akiyoshi impresses with a firm demeanor that is fully concentrated on eliciting the sounds she wants from the sixteen pieces before her. A meticulous craftswoman, she communicates precisely, using her whole body to speak for her" (168). The bashful, kimono-clad "Japanese little girl" from *What's My Line?* was gone when the band was roaring, replaced by a confident woman whose mastery of the ensemble was unmistakable. In a word, she was undeniably cool (see Figure 3.2).

Figure 3.2: *Lew Tabackin and Toshiko Akiyoshi, Tokyo, February 1979. Photo by K. Abe/Shinko Music/Getty Images.*

4 The Record

Like books and black lives, albums still matter.
PRINCE, FIFTY-SEVENTH ANNUAL GRAMMY AWARDS, FEBRUARY 8, 2015

The fledgling TA-LTBB had been rehearsing for several months when an old acquaintance, Isaka Hiroshi, head of the classical music division of RCA Records' Japan branch, contacted Akiyoshi about recording her big band. Isaka had produced her 1971 quartet album, *The Personal Aspect in Jazz*. He enlisted Kawashima Fumimaru, head of the Western popular music division and a big-band enthusiast, to handle promotion (Zen'on 2004, 101).

Kogun was recorded on April 3 and 4, 1974, at Sage and Sound, a small, eight-track studio in Hollywood. The budget was a mere $3200, a small amount even for 1974. "The guys in the band didn't even expect to get paid," Tabackin (2023) says. "We *did* pay them, not enough, but we *paid* them. They were surprised." Aside from the leaders, the lineup was as follows:

Tenor saxophone—Tom Peterson
Alto saxophones—Gary Foster, Dick Spencer
Baritone saxophone—Bill Perkins
Trumpets—Bobby Shew, John Madrid, Don Rader, Mike Price
Trombones—Charles Loper, Jim Sawyer, Britt Woodman, and
    Phil Teele (bass)

Bass—Gene Cherico
Drums—Peter Donald

Kogun (RCA-6246) was released in Japan in October 1974, its first pressing selling an astonishing (for a jazz album) 30,000 copies. *Down Beat* reviewed *Kogun* in 1976, when it was available in the United States only by mail order directly from the artists. RCA did not release it in the United States (AFL1-3019) until 1978, with alternate cover art by Dennis Pohl derived from Katsushika Hokusai's 1831 woodblock print *Under the Wave off Kanagawa* and a superfluous macron spelling the title *Kōgun*. After enthusiastic concert and record reviews and Grammy nominations for *Long Yellow Road* (1975), *Tales of a Courtesan* (1976), and the live double LP *Road Time* (1976), RCA conceded there was some American demand for the TA-LTBB's debut recording, but only after some prodding from Tabackin. "They thought it was too far out. So they released *Long Yellow Road* first, because to them it was less 'adventurous.' . . . They didn't try to sell it. They released [*Kogun*] under obligation." Akiyoshi pointed to different marketing practices in Japan and the United States: "There's no way to lose money on this band. Our monetary outlay in terms of production is moderate, but American companies are not interested in a moderate profit" (Rothbart 1980, 62) (see Figure 4.1).

Only one of the original five songs Akiyoshi brought to the initial rehearsals, "Henpecked Old Man," appears on *Kogun*; other pieces from the 1967 recital were reserved for later albums ("Let's Roll in Sake," an attempt at boogaloo funk from the *Top of the Gate* album, didn't last long: "We played it and it

Figure 4.1: *Cover for the Japanese release. Photo by Abe Katsuji.*

sucked," Shew chuckles, "so she threw it out of the book real fast"). Once the weekly rehearsals began and the band was beginning to cohere, she started writing new material. Mike Price explains that after she drove her husband and daughter to their respective destinations, she had most of the day to write and obviously made good use of the time. Whether or not she composed all the newer pieces in 1973–4, she was writing new arrangements for them, with individual bandsmen in mind, as became her custom.

* * *

Kogun opens with the hard-bop swinger "Elegy," composed in 1959 and titled "Toshiko's Elegy" and "My Elegy" on other albums. Recall that in his review of the first Ice House show, Leonard Feather had said that the band's "principal strength" was "Toshiko's mastery of the piano," so he was surely pleased with the composer's decision to begin with a solo. "Since this was our first recording," she said in Feather's liner notes to the American edition, "I thought it would be appropriate to begin with something featuring me at the piano."

Throughout her three decades as a bandleader, Akiyoshi gave herself little space for piano solos. Because "a jazz musician's happiest time is playing a solo," she explained, "to play with a big band is a second choice for a musician. And if I played a solo, I will have taken someone else's solo spot" (Kelly 2013, 233–4). Woodman, Spencer, and Tabackin take extended solo turns on "Elegy," accompanied by the rhythm section with only occasional input from the rest of the band. The ensemble passages illustrate Akiyoshi's distinctive placement of accents, which reflect "the influence of the Japanese concept of *ma*, which concerns the use of space, on her musical sensibilities" (Fellezs 2010, 52).

In his 1976 *Down Beat* review, Pete Welding compared this version of "Elegy" to an earlier rendition on the 1961 LP *Toshiko Mariano Quartet*, writing that it "is taken at what I feel is too brisk a pace. Consequently, it is a bit sloppy in execution (though it has a nicely spirited feel as compensation) and is, in comparison with the balance of the writing on the album, rather conventional sounding."[1]

* * *

The second track, "Memory," is a feature for Shew's mellifluous flugelhorn and one of Akiyoshi's inventive combinations: four flutes, bass clarinet, and bucket-muted trombone. As was true of Ellington's orchestra, listeners can immediately identify Akiyoshi's writing from the reed section alone. Rather than doubling some parts, she often writes five-part vertical harmonies. The four- or five-flute choir is arguably her most distinctive orchestral voice (Rothbart 1980, 15).

Yet "Memory" was somewhat controversial for including a studio-altered prerecorded voiceover tape by actor and radio personality Scott Ellsworth (b. 1927), something common enough in post-Beatles pop but almost never done in jazz. From 1970 to 1972, Ellsworth hosted a live jazz program, *Scott's Place*, on KFI AM-640 from 12:00 a.m. to 4:00 a.m. six nights a week. "I had Scott pick up some lines from the poetry of D.H. Lawrence," Akiyoshi explained to Feather. "I asked him to read them, and from that I picked words that I thought appropriate for this piece. I cut the tape[s] and kind of messed them up, wrinkled them, used echo on some, and re-recorded it." She spliced the tape into seven clips (four of which are only one or two seconds) and scattered them throughout the ten-minute composition; collectively, they total fifty-seven seconds.

Still, RCA executives wanted them removed, and some critics and listeners thought they detracted from the beauty of the music. Welding described "Memory" as a "lovely, delicate mood piece whose shimmering textures and colorations recall Gil Evans without, however, being specifically imitative."

The only thing marring what is otherwise a standout piece is the use of electronically altered speech sounds over the lambent theme, obscuring rather than adding to the music. Still, it indicates something of the provocative and striving nature of Toshiko's writing: she'd rather take a chance than play it safe. Even if it doesn't always work, I say amen to that.

Remembrance, of course, has been one of Akiyoshi's abiding thematic concerns. She explained to Feather, "as time goes by, what one remembers, or wants to remember, may be different from what really happened. I have tried to capture that feeling of distance from reality." Akiyoshi has been consistently critical of self-congratulatory narratives of Japanese national history, the "successes" of which came at the sacrifice of a great many people who had little to no say in the building of the modern nation-state. She realizes that there are (at least) two pasts: one that happened (elusive as its details may be to nail down), and one that's remembered. The critique in much of her work is not just of historical crimes, follies, or injustices, but also of pasts remembered and narrated uncritically, incompletely, and disingenuously.

If the underlying music of "Memory" suggests a pleasantly nostalgic recollection, the excerpts of Ellsworth's narration mimic fragments of intrusive (repressed?) memories that disrupt casual reminiscence without critical reflection. These fragments are distorted, clipped, and barely intelligible yet insistent. If they detract from the music, as some say, I contend that is precisely the composer's intention. Feather may have been correct that the tape effects "symboliz[e] the tricks played by our memory," but given Akiyoshi's penchant for telling stories that others have either overlooked or deliberately quashed, they might also represent the shards of uncomfortable, suppressed historical truths cutting through our thoughtless reveries.

* * *

"American Ballad" was a feature written specifically for one of the band's ringers, former Ellington trombonist Britt Woodman. Welding regarded Woodman as an "appropriate choice if ever there was one, as the composition is an evocation of Duke Ellington's characteristically full-bodied, uncloyingly romantic way with a melody—and he turns in a fine, big, blowsy reading of the lovely theme." He plays the noticeably Ellingtonian melody freely, ad libbing during measures 37–44 over just the rhythm section, and measures 53–6 with the woodwinds and 57–60 with brass behind him (Akiyoshi 1979a).

There are four instrument changes in the woodwind section throughout the piece. "I think Toshiko's use of woodwinds on this particular work was the beginning of something very special," Tabackin commented in the American release's sleeve notes. "Her unique way of voicing the woodwinds in five-part harmony—using two flutes, two clarinets and bass clarinet, with just bass and drums underneath—is highly individual, and it's employed here both as background behind Britt, and also as a woodwind soli effect" (measures 46–52). Welding concurred: "The writing is especially pretty, with a delicious use of woodwinds throughout."

* * *

Kogun closes with the blues swinger "Henpecked Old Man." Composed in 1964 during her Japan sojourn with Mariano, it contains a melodic fragment from "Yagi bushi," a folkloric dance song from the Jōshū region north of Tokyo (Gunma, Tochigi, and Saitama prefectures) performed for the Bon homecoming festival (August 13–16), during which ancestral spirits are visited and venerated.

"Yagi bushi" was one of the first regional folksongs (*min'yō*) to become widely known at the dawn of the recording era. The melody came from a late-nineteenth-century narrative song (*kudoki uta*) sung by maids (*meshimori onna*) who served clients at local inns, one of which was called Yagi-shuku. It became a local Bon dance favorite when one Asakura Seizō gave it a crisp, galloping rhythm. Tochigi entertainer Horigome Genta (1872–1943) popularized it in the 1910s with a recording and live performances in Tokyo's Asakusa entertainment district (Saitō 2014, 41; Provine et al. 2001, 637–8).

Feather's notes say the melody is from a village "supposedly noted for its henpecked men and cold winds." The common term for "henpecked husband" is *nyōbō tenka* ("wife is heaven"); however, the composition likely refers more specifically to the local Jōshū phenomenon of *kakaadenka*, a household in which the wife's authority supersedes the husband's. As managers of Jōshū's sericulture industry, women were often the principal breadwinners, giving them more status in their households than was the norm elsewhere. Gunma prefecture proudly presents this as a unique, indigenous tradition of female empowerment in a predominantly patriarchal society.[2]

The Japanese references in "Henpecked Old Man" are easily missed, though: its basic form is a twelve-bar blues showcasing extended solos by Tabackin, Shew, and Spencer (at over twenty-one minutes, the live version on *Road Time* allows plenty more solo space). The theme based on "Yagi bushi" does not appear until the last minute of the piece, although Tabackin quotes it in his solo as well.

Welding called the closer "a crisp cooker, offering nothing profound but full of exuberant, invigoratingly rhythmic playing. It is a fine way to end the album." *Kogun* thus concludes with a bluesy barnburner that, along with "Elegy," would please big-band enthusiasts who might have found the other tracks too unconventional.

* * *

Kogun's commercial performance far surpassed all expectations. A jazz record was considered successful if it sold ten thousand copies; *Kogun* sold three times that in Japan (Zen'on 2004, 102). These sales were remarkable at a time when jazz-rock fusion was dominating the market, especially considering that traditional jazz fans generally didn't care for either big bands or Japanese musical elements in their jazz (Tabackin 2023). Akiyoshi expected derision from "purists" in Japan. "I thought, 'Go ahead and put me down, I really don't care.'" When *Kogun* became an "all-time seller," "I was surprised, because my records *never* sold!" (Monterey Jazz Festival 2016).

Kogun also earned near-universal critical praise in Japan and the United States.[3] Prominent jazz critics Yui Shōichi (1918–98) and Segawa Masahisa (1924–2021) each gave the record the *Swing Journal* equivalent of a five-star review in *Down Beat*, a cartoon of a dapper movie director doffing his hat with a bow. Both men had watched Akiyoshi's growth since the 1950s and could scarcely contain their pride in her.[4] *Kogun* won *Swing Journal*'s Eighth Silver Disc Award (edged out for the Gold Disc by Keith Jarrett's *Solo Concerts: Bremen/Lausanne*). In his essay on the award, Yui pointed out that *Kogun* had been *his* choice for the Gold Disc and that Jarrett's record had not even been in his top ten.[5]

In December 1974, two months after the album's release, Akiyoshi, Tabackin, bassist Bob Daugherty, and drummer Bill Goodwin embarked on a triumphal three-week tour of Japan.[6] For the December 4 performance at Tokyo's Yomiuri Hall, they assembled an orchestra of Japanese musicians to play pieces from *Kogun*.[7] On December 19, Akiyoshi produced her husband's first album as a leader, *Let the Tape Roll* (RCA 6271).

They were just getting started.

5   The Title Track

The world is all a dream, and he who wakes, casting it from him, may yet know the real.
RENSHŌ, IN *ATSUMORI* BY ZEAMI MOTOKIYO (THE-NOH.COM)

Historically, when jazz musicians from Japan or elsewhere entered the sights of the American jazz community, they encountered presumptions that to be original, they must draw on or evoke music from their homelands; if their ethno-national identities weren't aurally apparent, they were deemed "derivative." *Down Beat*'s review of Akiyoshi's debut album expressed disappointment that such culturally reductive "orientalist expectations" (Atkins 2001, 30) were not met: "Toshiko's two originals . . . are about as Japanese as Barbara Carroll." The album cover drawing by David Stone Martin—which features a willowy "Toshiko" in a form-fitting Chinese "dragon lady" (or Morticia Addams?) dress and an ikebana flower arrangement on her piano—partially sated the reviewer's desire for the exotic. The music earned three stars, the artwork five.[1]

Deborah Wong (2004) describes the dilemma facing American-born musicians of Asian descent: "The risk of reinscription, appropriation, or orientalist misreading is ever present in Asian American performance; the possibility of empowerment stands side by side with the susceptible audience that consumes with the greedy expectation of orientalist pleasure and is inevitably gratified" (7). Artists striving to create unique voices and attract audiences must decide whether to engage in "auto-exoticism" as a strategy for garnering recognition and acceptance (Manabe 2013). Tamara Roberts observes that composer/saxophonist Fred Ho's use of Asian instruments, legends, kung fu imagery, and song titles "opens up the possibility for misinterpretations" that mark him as a "perpetual foreigner." She ponders if they "paint Ho and his work as Other to the United States and simplify and conflate traditions with vastly different national origins and cultural contexts into a singular performed Orient" (Buckley and Roberts 2013, 9–10).

For Akiyoshi, composing with reference to Japanese musical traditions (collectively known as *hōgaku*) was both liberating and empowering, not pandering. It was, as Tabackin puts it, "organic," but also intentional and restrained, like Ellington's expressions of racial pride. Moreover, compared to most other artists engaged in similar efforts in Japan, she was raised with more intimate knowledge of some *hōgaku* genres because of her father's and sister Hisako's interests in *nō* and traditional dance, respectively. Yet her music was not intended to be a mnemonic device for representing or essentializing "Japan" for non-Japanese audiences; she used it to craft a singular, individual voice, as jazz aesthetics demands of top-tier performers. It was not, however, her only musical signature, just one of several devices that distinguish her voice from that of other composer/arrangers.

Jazz musicians in Japan had been incorporating indigenous music sporadically since the late 1930s. Composer/arrangers Hattori Ryōichi (1907–33), Sugii Kōichi (1906–42), and Sano

Tasuku (1908–96) released recordings of Japanese and Chinese folksongs to deflect ultranationalists' critiques and avoid censorship by the wartime state (Atkins 2001, 132–9; Atkins 2018). In the mid-1960s, eager to impress overseas audiences with something original, drummer Shiraki Hideo (1933–72) and saxophonist Hara Nobuo's (1926–2021) Sharps and Flats Big Band performed indigenous repertoire with *hōgaku* instrumentalists: Shiraki with a trio of *koto* (zither) players in West Germany; and Hara with *shakuhachi* player Yamamoto Hōzan (1937–2014) and an entire set of *min'yō* at the Newport Jazz Festival. Others spoke of nurturing a national style (*Nihonteki jazu*) "that only Japanese could play." For them, individuality and national style were not mutually exclusive but rather facilitated each other's development (Atkins 2001, 241–8; Hosokawa 2007).

Yet most jazz aficionados in Japan did not care for such blends, finding them contrived, a dilution of the art's essential African American character, and pandering to the international audience's craving for exotica (a charge frequently leveled against filmmaker Kurosawa Akira for his samurai movies). Akiyoshi anticipated such criticism (Nishida 2019, 74; Tabackin 2023), which made *Kogun*'s critical reception and initial sales figures even more remarkable.

When Akiyoshi arrived at Berklee, school director Lawrence Berk stated, "Until now, we have had no Oriental influence in jazz. I sincerely feel that she's it. She is going to contribute considerably to the further development of the idiom. She's just alive with musical imagination."[2] Akiyoshi began composing and arranging Japan-themed songs as early as her second album, *The Toshiko Trio*. She used the Japanese term for "homesickness" to entitle her composition "Kyōshū (Nostalgia)." "Soshū no yoru" ("Suzhou Nocturne") was a China-themed pop song (*kayōkyoku*) written by prolific songsmiths Saijō Yaso and Hattori Ryōichi in 1940, one of many "continental melodies" (*tairiku merodī*) that romanticized Asian locales the military was then invading and bombing to hell.[3]

Later compositions such as "The Village" (1961) and "Henpecked Old Man" (1964) included passages quoting folkloric melodies ("Kisarazu jinku" and "Yagi bushi," respectively). She later described "Sumi-e" (the term for monochrome ink painting), which debuted at the 1967 Town Hall recital, as her first serious attempt at an Ellingtonian evocation of her "roots" (Nishida, 2019, 93). But these were "subtle infusions" (Feather 1976, 17), nestled within dense harmonies, complex rhythms, and unconventional song forms. Most non-Japanese listeners were hipped to their folkloric origins only by the titles or liner notes. Akiyoshi seldom played such material "straight" enough to be gimmicky or pigeonholed as stereotypically "oriental." Her fluency in bebop was more conspicuous.

"Kogun" was easily her most audacious attempt to date at a "blend" (*yūgō*) of jazz and *hōgaku* (Akiyoshi 1996, 208–9) (it was also arguably the most convincing, natural-sounding such combination since Sugii Kōichi's sublime wartime jazz renditions of East Asian folksongs).[4] The composition (in E minor) has very few chord changes and thus could be considered modal.

Here, I confine my analysis to the "Japanese" section (A, A', and A") of the composition and Tabackin's flute playing. These are the aspects on which both musicians have commented most and have drawn the most attention, although not with

Table 1: Basic Form of "Kogun"

Section (to provide more detail, lettering does not conform with rehearsal markers in score)	Measures	Recording timestamp	Description
A ("Japanese" section)	1–31	0:00–1:33	Begins with *kakegoe*, *tsuzumi*, Tabackin's flute, and *gagaku*-like glissandi; eleven measures repeated twice, with several metrical changes (3/4 > 4/4 > 2/4 > 3/4) (see Figure 5.2).
B	32–41	1:34–1:58	Swung 5/4 meter; Tabackin plays new melody over sparse brass punches.
A'	42–51	1:59–2:25	
C	53–105, with lead-in from 52	2:26–3:50	Through-composed swung passage over E minor, with occasional A7 chords on beats three and four of every other bar under a partial restatement of section A melody (measures 76–85); then complex triplet and sixteenth-note figures in woodwinds (flute, alto saxophone, alto clarinet, two soprano saxophones) with brass accents.
D	N/A	3:51–5:37	Improvised flute cadenza.
B'	109–18	5:38–6:00	
A"	119–32	6:01–6:47	

the same degree of contextualization and reference to *nō* and *gagaku* aesthetics used here.

Akiyoshi confirmed to me that the composition eventually entitled "Kogun," including its *nō* and *gagaku* elements, was already under development when she heard the news of Lt. Onoda's surrender. It was originally intended primarily as a feature for her husband's flute. Yet fortuitously, the narrative conventions and thematic concerns of *nō* made it an ideal medium for conveying the pathos of his story. Most *nō* plays are tragedies, and she clearly regarded Onoda's experience as such. She may have admired his hardiness as others did, but she regarded war as senseless and lamented the brainwashing that prolonged his ordeal and caused unspeakable suffering for so many others (Akiyoshi 1996, 21–2).

Classic *nō* blends the supernatural with the historical, exploring the karmic ramifications of the protagonist's past actions and delusions. Plays often feature historical figures and events, interpreting their contemporary significance in both the material and spirit worlds. I contend that Akiyoshi's deployment of *kakegoe* vocals and *tsuzumi* drums effectively reimagines Lt. Onoda's story as a *nō* play: an allegory about a warrior's delusion and madness, and his spirit's disorienting journey between worlds. Beneath Tabackin's flute melody, she also spreads a sonic tapestry laden with the signature glissando of *gagaku*, the majestic and mysterious music of the imperial court, which I maintain heightens the tension and sense of instability. Her "blend" is not just of African American and traditional Japanese music but of jazz with two distinct *hōgaku* genres, each with its own history, purpose, aural textures, and symbolic meanings.

The fact that she dedicated the piece to Onoda after its basic concept was in place does not necessarily invalidate this reading; in fact, it is likely that initially "Kogun" was a story without a *shite*—the principal actor/dancer/protagonist in a *nō* play (usually the guy wearing the mask)—and that Akiyoshi recognized in Onoda attributes of some of the genre's canonical characters and scenarios. As a self-described narrative or programmatic composer, she had created an appropriate format for a story of which she only became aware during the writing process. The timing is less important than the suitability of the narrative style to the story.

The analysis that follows ventures beyond what Akiyoshi has written or said publicly about the design of "Kogun" to unpack additional layers of meaning in the "blend" she was crafting. Whether intentional or not, these layers are meaningful: the beauty of any art is finding meaning that transcends authorial purpose or design, and as a student of Japanese culture, I detect symbolism in the use of *nō* and *gagaku* in "Kogun" that I hope will enrich appreciation of this magisterial piece.

* * *

Nō originated in the fourteenth century, evolving from folk antecedents known as *sarugaku* ("monkey music") and *dengaku* ("field music") to become the theatrical form patronized by Japan's warrior aristocracy. As its name suggests, *sarugaku* was more playful than its somber theatrical offspring, featuring acrobats, jugglers, puppet shows, dancers, and comedy (the more humorous attributes survive in *kyōgen*, short comic sketches interspersed between *nō* plays to lighten the mood). Enraptured by a *sarugaku* performance by actor/playwright

Kan'ami Kiyotsugu (1333–84) and his eleven-year-old son Zeami Motokiyo (1363–1443), *shōgun* Ashikaga Yoshimitsu (1358–1408) became their troupe's patron. Building on his father's ideas and practices, Zeami wrote plays as well as treatises that outline *nō*'s aesthetic ideals and performance techniques. Although there are a handful of styles (*ryū*) and artistic lineages (*iemoto* or *mon*) that originated in medieval and early modern times, these are typically rooted in interpretations of Zeami's principles. In "Kogun" and other compositions incorporating *nō* elements, Akiyoshi employs styles from the Kanze *ryū* that her father had studied, the oldest of the five main *nō* schools, dating back to the fourteenth century (the name "Kanze" combines the first ideographs of the names of the father-son team who founded canonical *nō*) (Kanze.net).

The Chinese ideograph for *nō* means "talent," "skill," and "ability," and everyone involved in a production undergoes decades of training to master their respective roles. *Nō* combines many different types of artistry (each with its own *ryū*): acting, dancing, vocal and instrumental music, prose and poetic literature, and visual art (masks, costuming, and stage design). It makes frequent allusions to Shintō folk religion, Buddhism, Chinese and Japanese history and legends, and canonical literature. For newbies, there is an illusion of simplicity that obscures its technical complexity and emotional and thematic depth.

It can take an hour to perform an eight- to ten-page script, and one often sees people dozing at a performance. *Nō* doesn't shoot for the quick dopamine rush but rather for *yūgen*, profound insight or awareness of the plight of humankind and our relationships with the natural and supernatural worlds. *Yūgen* is a Zen concept for sensitivity to "what lies beneath the surface," "the subtle as opposed to the obvious; the hint, as opposed to the statement" (Waley 1921, 21). Like many other traditional arts, *nō* elicits active contemplation, quasi-mystical experiences, and emotional revelations that cannot be articulated in words (Yasuda 2021, 52–3, 79).

Nō includes instrumental music, performed by the *hayashi* (usually three percussion instruments and one transverse *nōkan* flute), and highly stylized vocal parts (*utai*) divided among the *shite* and a group of singers (*jiutai*), which is often likened to a Greek chorus in that it reacts to and comments on the action. *Kakegoe* are single syllables (*yo*, *ho*, *iya*, etc.) voiced by the *tsuzumi* drummers as musical cues to establish and change tempo and mood, and thus are distinct from *utai* song texts, which have long been performed separately in social gatherings by professionals and amateur enthusiasts (Fujita 2019, 228–30; Yasuda 2021, 27–8, 39–41).

A *hayashi* typically includes a *taiko* drum played with sticks and two hourglass-shaped *tsuzumi* played by hand. The larger *ōtsuzumi* is placed at the drummer's hip, the smaller *kotsuzumi* on the shoulder. Each drummer has distinct *kakegoe* that they shout between strokes; the vocalizations sometimes "fill" the interval between the final beat of an eight-beat cycle and the first beat of the next (Fujita 2019, 218); and they also help the musicians coordinate as they follow the dancer. Their tonal quality and length depend on the context: they are "strict," shorter shouts for a steady, regular pulse, or "flexible," longer melismatic howls when the tempo is more elastic. Both types are heard at the beginning of "Kogun."

Figure 5.1: Hayashi *onstage (l to r): Mochizuki Takinojō II* (shimedaiko), *Katada Kisaburō V* (ōtsuzumi), *Kawashima Yūsuke* (kotsuzumi), *and Fukuhara Hyakushichi* (nōkan). *Photograph by Kagawa Kenji, courtesy of Sonica Instruments, https://sonica.jp. As a member of the Katada ryū, Kisaburō studied with Kisaku III, who performed "Kogun" with the TA-LTBB at a 1976 concert documented on* Road Time.

In addition to its cueing function, *kakegoe* is a gathering and release of energy before a drum strike and helps musicians synchronize their breathing (*komi*). *Komi* is a silent abdominal breath, "a sharp rhythmic inhale," taken before the drumming pattern begins. "After the build-up of internal energy through the *komi*, a vocal call breaks the silence and leads to a release by a strike" (Noh Intermedia). When commenting on the *kakegoe* part in "Kogun," Akiyoshi has specifically mentioned this function, which she essentially applied to her orchestra. The recorded shouts, howls, and drums are not merely ancillary effects: when Tabackin's flute and the ensemble enter, it becomes clear that the *kakegoe* and *tsuzumi* have established the pulse and mood for the first section of the piece. Voice and drum continue throughout section A, the melismatic vocals paralleling and amplifying the glissando effect produced by a truly unique orchestral combination (discussed below). Thus, what may initially strike some listeners as incongruence between *hayashi* and jazz ensembles eventually proves to be seamless integration.

With such a small budget to record *Kogun*, bringing *tsuzumi* drummers from Japan for the session was out of the question. So, as with "Memory," Akiyoshi edited a prerecorded tape, painstakingly syncing it with what the band had already recorded. Tabackin (2023) recalls:

> So what she did, which was kind of remarkable, she took a demonstration tape of *tsuzumi* drums and spent hours in the studio with an engineer with a razor blade . . . putting together the drum line, the percussion line that she heard, and it took a lot of patience. . . . And then when eventually we got to play it with real *tsuzumi* players [in concert] . . . , they were impressed by the fact that what she put together was, you know, the right shit. It wasn't like accidental: she had really figured out the line and it was very natural for them to do what basically she had done.

It is difficult for those of us uninitiated in the intricacies of *nō* to appreciate the precision with which the *kakegoe* and *tsuzumi* rhythmic patterns were incorporated. Few listeners, even Japanese, would have known if it were the "wrong shit." Akiyoshi's meticulous efforts to edit the tape properly, to the satisfaction of real *nō* musicians, are impressive, indicating the strength of her concept, the depth of her bimusicality, and her reverence for that tradition. The tape was no randomly pasted-on artifice but was as essential to the composition as any other part and required the same degree of care.

Rather than incorporating a full four-piece *hayashi*, Akiyoshi recorded only the *tsuzumi* drummers and their vocal cries. She assigned the main melody to her husband's sonorous metallic flute, which had inspired the composition in the first place (in *nō*, the flute's main function is to mark "poignant parts," entrances, exits, and transitions in a play; the primary melody is the *utai*) (Anno 2020, 1, 98–9). Tabackin was hesitant: with the exceptions of Frank Wess and James Moody, he says, "I wasn't a great fan of jazz flute . . . I said, 'Toshiko, I don't want to do some kind of bebop flute solo; that'd be kind of stupid. Tell me [Onoda's] story . . . I can try to make a narrative statement.' . . . That was the beginning of my approach to that kind of playing." The challenge of this assignment fundamentally transformed Tabackin's flute concept. "Why should I play the same stuff I play on saxophone on the flute? Most people do that when they double. So I decided not to 'double,' [but] to *separate* like the yin and the yang. I'm separating like the male and the female. . . . It's like a schizophrenic approach" (Tabackin 2023).

According to jazz flute master James Newton, because flutes are found in music cultures around the world, it is not uncommon for players "to look to the performance techniques of other cultures that play non-Western, indigenous flutes, and to adapt aspects of these performance practices to the Western instrument. When I use *glissandi* on the flute, my inspiration may come from Billie Holiday, Johnny Hodges or the *shakuhachi* artistry of [Watazumi] Doso" (Westbrook 2011, x–xi).

Illustrating Newton's point, Tabackin listened intently to Japanese flute music before (and after) recording "Kogun," trying "to absorb what I heard in an organic way" (2023). He considers the flute universal because it is primordial: "The flute is a first instrument. It . . . exists in nature, even without playing it—just the wind blowing through a reed" (Westbrook 2011, 305). Since most jazz flutists are "doublers," and Akiyoshi "hated all these saxophone players who played lousy flute," he had a high standard to meet. He had a solid foundation in Western concert flute, having studied in conservatory with Murray Panitz (1925–89), principal flute for the Philadelphia Orchestra. Particularly with regard to tonal concepts, his main flute influences were in the European concert and Japanese *hōgaku* traditions, rather than in jazz. "I want the sound to influence the line and it doesn't necessarily lend itself to a 'bebop' kind of playing," Tabackin confesses. "[T]he better I got at playing the flute, the worse it was to play the stylistic jazz flute at the time" (Westbrook 2011, 302–5; see also Feather 1978a, 16).

Tabackin uses fingering techniques and microtonal slurs from Japanese flute practices. For instance, players of the end-blown *shakuhachi* use the *meri-kari* technique (combining "half-holing" with adjustments to embouchure) to play quarter tones between the main pitches D, F, G, A, and D (Malm 1959, 159). But the roundness of Tabackin's tone, frequently likened to the *shakuhachi*'s, is what sets his playing apart from that of other jazz flutists. What he calls the "one-note concept" from *shakuhachi* music meshed with Tabackin's longstanding concern with sonority. "I could play one note a hundred different ways. . . . Say, if I play a low E, display it, play it again, play it a little differently, change the pitch a little bit, eventually I'm like in some kind of a trance—I go into another world of not thinking" (Westbrook 2011, 305).

Yet replicating *shakuhachi* is only one facet of his "Japanese" playing. Depending on the context, he also mimics the more piercing sound (*hishigi*) of the *nōkan*. *Shakuhachi* and *nōkan* each have approximately two-and-a-half-octave ranges: when calculated in equal temperament (A = 440 Hz), a standard 1.8 *shaku* (54.5 cm), five-hole *shakuhachi* generally ranges from D4 to G6, whereas the 1.29 *shaku* (39 cm), seven-hole *nōkan* is pitched higher (approximately D#5 to F#6). Figure 5.3 shows that Tabackin plays the main theme of "Kogun" in the higher *nōkan* register, ranging from E5 to A7. In section B and his improvisation, he plays in a lower register with a fatter tone that more resembles *shakuhachi*.[5]

Figure 5.2: *Lew Tabackin at Brecon Jazz Festival, Wales, 1995. Photo by David Redfern/Redferns/Getty Images.*

When playing in an "Asian" mode, Tabackin (2023) explains, he is not thinking like a jazz musician—indeed, he's not really thinking at all.

> It's almost a Zen kind of thing: play one note many different ways, with many different nuances. . . . I get into one note, and it would tell me what to do . . .
>
> I can get hypnotized, kind of get out of my thinking stage. And I just play. It might be one minute, ten minutes, I don't know . . . But when it's over, it's over.

When he first played "Kogun," in concert in Tokyo, Tabackin worried the audience would think he was "jive." Instead, people told him, "You have a Japanese soul."

* * *

Both Tabackin and Akiyoshi consider themselves storytellers. It is one of the traits that each admires most in the other and that has cemented their artistic partnership. Her oeuvre consists of several programmatic compositions that tell stories through sound and inspire reflection on extramusical matters.

> In my mind, it's very important to tell a story. My music has to have a certain attitude, it must reflect my view of certain things—that's what I like to bring into the music I write—a point of view. That's the difference between a writer and an arranger. Duke was a writer, his music told stories.[6]

Tabackin's aspiration to be a "narrative player" in his improvisations complements his wife's concept. Her arrangements leave space for him to accentuate moods and dramatize the story. Although her *Minamata* and *Hiroshima* suites include spoken-word segments, she prefers to weave tales wordlessly: "What's good about instrumental music is that it's not like a lyric," which "designates" or delimits meaning (Kelly 2013, 235).

As stated earlier, in "Kogun," the narrative mode for Onoda's story comes from *nō*, which not only recounted legends and conveyed spiritual truths but was also a medium for historical interpretation: plays presented karmic cause-and-effect relationships between the past and present and thus could shape collective remembering of people and events. There are underlying congruities between his story and the thematic concerns and narrative tropes of the *nō* tradition.

Nō plays are categorized as either *mugen* (phantasmic) or *genzai* (present-day), although these frequently overlap. There are five subcategories in which the *shite* is a god, man, woman, deranged person, or demon. With reference to these categories, I argue that "Kogun" evokes elements from both *mugen* and *genzai* plays, specifically the subcategories "man" about tormented warriors (*shura mono*) and "insanity" plays (*kurui* or *kyōran mono*).

Nō was "born when men felt the gods as living beings in close proximity to them." *Mugen* plays take place within the liminal space between the material world and the spiritual realm, where the main protagonist has dreams or visions revealing the present ramifications and consequences of prior actions. When actors emerge from the so-called "mirror room" (the backstage area where the *shite* dons his mask) and walk the bridge (*hashigakari*) to the main stage, they traverse time and space between realms (Ishii 1994, 43, 53).

Igarashi argues that when Yokoi Shōichi, Onoda Hiroo, and Nakamura Teruo emerged from their respective hiding places in the early 1970s, they were moving in both space and time: from geographical locations once nominally "Japanese" by military conquest to a much more narrowly constructed "Japan"; and from a past in which *bushidō*-inspired martial masculinity and the sanctity of the emperor were unquestioned values to a present in which those were discredited, outmoded, and irrelevant. The survival and repatriation of these three castaway soldiers complicated the geographical and temporal demarcation between "prewar" (*senzen*) and "postwar" (*sengo*) Japan (Igarashi 2016, 224).

The soldiers navigated the liminal space between the (lost) empire and homeland, between the past and present, under intense public scrutiny. They were "ghostly figures" who "had returned from a netherworld to settle the account with the war dead." Observers struggled to find meaning in their existence. When elderly people met with Yokoi, one magazine reported, they were "meeting with their loved ones lost in the war, by using Mr. Yokoi, who came back from the netherworld, as a medium" (Igarashi 2016, 149, 169). In essence, the public was watching a *nō* play in which the returnees were the afflicted *shite*, trying to discern lessons and find illumination— to experience *yūgen*—in their anguish.

The haunted warrior is a venerable figure in *nō*. In *shura* (from the Sanskrit *asura*, demigods opposed to the Vedic *devas*) plays, warriors face karmic retribution for lives of violence; they depict "the ghosts of defeated warriors who recount their last battles on earth and their sufferings in the *asura* realm [*shuradō*, warrior hell] of Buddhist cosmology" (Sekine 1985,

9). Canonical works typically focus on actual historical figures whose exploits are recounted (and embellished) in *Tale of the Heike*, a martial epic based on the Genpei War (1185–92). For instance, the titular protagonist in Zeami's *Sanemori* chants:

> Although I was submerged like a buried log to which the world gives no thought, please allow me to completely repent my numerous unspeakable sufferings as a warrior in the realm of Asuras before I will attain buddhahood. My deeds were beyond words. (The-Noh.com)

In *Yorimasa*, the *shite* wanders about in spiritual limbo, unable to traverse from one realm to the next:

> Because of my worldly attachments, I have been floating up and down on the waves, unable to cross over to the world beyond. I will tell you the cause and effect of this karma. (The-Noh.com)

These *Heike* heroes express the disorientation and misery the three castaway soldiers appear to have experienced, which was less about the people they had killed than about the comrades they had lost and the failure of their missions. Yokoi—who famously said he was "embarrassed" to have survived—continued to have nightmares about being chased by the enemy and "to apologize to his war buddies for surviving alone" (Igarashi 2016, 171). Onoda swore vengeance against the Filipinos who shot his comrades, Shimada and Kozuka, which partially explains his aggression toward them. As an indigenous Taiwanese, Nakamura/Suniyon's ordeal was different and more pitiable: he had fled his squadron, convinced that his Japanese comrades would murder him; he was technically stateless, his Japanese citizenship revoked by the 1952 peace treaty; and as a former colonial subject, the Japanese media and public were not sure how, or if, to regard him. He returned to his village in Taiwan, able to speak Japanese, Amis, and some Hokkien, but no Mandarin, the official language mandated by Chiang Kai-shek's Nationalist regime. His wife had remarried, although she eventually reunited with him. Other castaway soldiers who had returned earlier had to pay their own medical expenses and worked low-wage construction jobs for decades (Trefalt 2003, 164–8; Igarashi 2016, 206–7). Like their forebears in *nō* plays, they were lost in post-warrior hell.

Madness (*kyōki* or *monogurui*) is another prevalent subject in *nō*. *Kurui/kyōran* plays feature a character (often but not always a woman) "who wanders about in mental distraction until she finds someone she has been looking for" (Shimazaki 1998, 49). Mikiko Ishii (1994) argues that Zeami saw derangement as an ideal lens for examining life. So fundamental is this subject to *shura* and *kurui* plays that there is even a designated "anguish dance" (*kakeri*), accompanied by a sudden increase in tempo, that signifies a state of madness.

Five subgroups of insanity plays are distinguished by the source or cause of insanity. Some characters, deranged by "exaggerated refinement," are "exceptionally sensitive and perceptive" and "become quite unbalanced when faced with a cruel fact of life." Given Akiyoshi's stated conviction that Onoda was misguided by wartime indoctrination, his story resembles plays that attribute madness to "over-refined sensibilities" (Ishii 1994, 60–1, 64), which aptly describes his remarkably tenacious attachment to the ideology of the imperial fascist state, something for which Onoda was admired by some and vilified by others.

Fascism deranges entire societies. As Akiyoshi herself suggested, to varying degrees, Onoda's entire generation succumbed to madness. Yet very few of the other military castaways who repatriated between 1945 and 1974 exhibited the same degree of self-delusion and continued enthusiasm for violence that Onoda did. He and Kozuka dismissed information from multiple sources (including their own family members) that would have convinced most others that the war had ended. And, most tragically, they continued to terrorize the people of Lubang with the same contemptuous impunity the Japanese military had consistently displayed wherever it landed (this being a music book, I will spare readers the gruesome details of what Onoda and Kozuka did to Acquerino de Lara on April 22, 1970; see Fujinami 1977, 121). His sensibilities "over-refined" by fascist brainwashing and his training in intelligence and "secret warfare," Onoda stood out among castaway soldiers for his zeal and conviction that his crimes against locals were justified because, as far as he knew, he was still at war (Igarashi 2016, 179–82).

Nō narratives frequently show how self-delusion (*mōshū*) leads to absurd thoughts and behaviors: folly and tragedy occur when people develop attachments (*shūchaku*) that reify what is not real.

> Please save me from the delusions of my attachments. —Teika, Konparu Zenchiku. (The-Noh.com)
>
> *How vain the tie made by delusion is.* —Tsunemasa, Zeami. (The-Noh.com)

Su Kwang-ha (1975) detects intriguing similarities between *nō* and post–Second World War "theatre of the absurd." A genre of European and American existentialist plays that drew attention to the "futility and pointlessness of human effort" and "irremediable character of the human condition," Martin Esslin (1960) contended that "the Theatre of the Absurd links up with an older tradition which has almost completely disappeared from Western culture: the tradition of allegory and the symbolical representation of abstract concepts personified [through] characters" (4–5, 15).

Though based on distinct philosophical foundations— European existentialism and Buddhist notions of the illusory nature of phenomenal reality (*makyō*)—both absurdist theater and *nō* "make use of mythical, allegorical, and dreamlike modes of thought; both use ritual and pure stylized action; both are anti-realistic and despise objectively valid characters; both provoke discontinuity of emotion" (Su 1975, 55–6). Protagonists "appear as mere marionettes, helpless puppets without any will of their own, passively at the mercy of blind fate and meaningless circumstance" and occupying "a world without faith, meaning, and genuine freedom of will" (Esslin 1960, 4–5). Describing Onoda and other soldiers as men with no control over their own fates (Monterey Jazz Festival 2016), Akiyoshi presented their experience as an existential problem.

While many admired Onoda, Yokoi, and Nakamura, others considered them absurd, "farcical figures" (Igarashi 2016, 170), even national embarrassments, for their attachments to wartime ideologies. Yokoi, who was repeatedly badgered with lurid questions about his libido and sexual behavior while in hiding (Omi 2009, 181–2; Igarashi 2016, 53–4), was viewed with more pity than admiration. "He is a living example of militarism," some said, "like a visitor from outer space." A newspaper poll showed sharp generational differences in admiration for Yokoi's dedication "to fight for the emperor," ranging from 15.6 percent of teenagers to 35 percent of those born during the war, and 84 percent of sexagenarians (Sankei Shinbun 1972, 135–6; Trefalt 2003, 182).

Onoda's account of his three decades in the Philippine jungle was met with everything "from enthusiasm to suspicion, accusations of mental instability, and even disloyalty." His ghostwriter, Tsuda Shin, testified that the memoir was "full of deception . . . and written for the purpose of justifying Onoda's actions." Although he apologized to President Marcos for "causing great trouble to the people of the Philippines," at other times he "maintained his aggressive stance against the Lubang locals and reenacted it in his interactions with the Japanese media," even threatening violence against one critic. His handler from the Ministry of Health and Welfare struggled to manage his tongue. Ultimately, Japanese "had little interest in a man who was still dragging the war along with him" (Igarashi 2016, 174, 189–97). By the end of 1974, after a quarrel with his parents, Onoda left Japan for Brazil, furious that he had not been more broadly welcomed as a hero. Faced with the consequences of his actions before and after repatriation, his homeland had become warrior hell.

In sum, by using *tsuzumi* and *kakegoe* in "Kogun," Akiyoshi presents Onoda's tale as a *nō* allegory, dramatizing the loneliness, pathos, and absurdity of his situation. Mimicking the dark sonority of the *shakuhachi*, Tabackin's plaintive flute cadenza accentuates his isolation, confusion, and disorientation. Through careful editing, she integrated the *tsuzumi* and *kakegoe* so that they retained their original functions, setting the mood and tempo for the orchestra. As the narrator, she casts Onoda as the *shite* in a play that draws from both the *shura* and *kurui* categories, presenting him as a sympathetic but delusional figure whose attachment to wartime ideology was calamitous yet whose fate was ultimately beyond his control.

* * *

The *nō* elements of "Kogun" are obvious; less so are those from *gagaku*. Stowe (2006) and Fellezs (2010) have noted them but not explored their meaning. In section A, Akiyoshi employs glissando, an essential melodic component of *gagaku*, perhaps to convey the instability and disorientation that Onoda, and Japanese society in general, experienced on his return.

Gagaku ("elegant music") is the orchestral music and dance of the imperial court. Like its Korean counterpart, *aak*, it is based partially on the ceremonial music of China's Tang Dynasty (618–907), brought home by diplomatic missions studying multiple aspects of Chinese statecraft to establish a centralized bureaucratic imperial administration in Japan. Although *gagaku* and *aak* infuse older indigenous repertoire and rituals specific to Japan and Korea, many musicologists regard them as the closest surviving approximations to ancient Chinese court music and possibly "the oldest extant orchestral art music in the world" (Malm 1959, 77).

The basic forms and conventions of *gagaku* were established in the tenth century. Instrumentation consists of wind (transverse flutes, mouth-blown reed organ *shō*, and the double-reed *hichiriki*), strings (lutes, zithers, and harps), and percussion (drums, gongs, and clappers). Depending on the purpose or occasion, it can be instrumental, vocal, or accompaniment to dance (*bugaku*). The top-tier musicians, dancers, and ensembles were employed by the imperial court, whose financial fortunes wavered over the course of centuries. With the restoration of the monarchy to de facto political power after 1868, the art was revived, and the ensemble standardized to three wind, three string, and two percussion instruments.

A canonical piece like *Etenraku* ("music brought from heaven") conveys moods that can be described as mysterious, majestic, ethereal, languorous, and otherworldly, symbolizing the attributes ascribed to the god-emperor. Today, there are hobbyists and civic groups that perform *gagaku*, but the Imperial Household Agency's Music Department continues to manage the official court orchestra, which performs at various ceremonies, state dinners, and on foreign tours (Kunaichō).

Musicologists have emphasized the centrality of glissando, performed by voice, *hichiriki*, and *shō*, to *gagaku* melodies, insisting it is not merely "ornamentation." "The use of microtones in gagaku and many other Asian musics is neither a decorative touch nor an ornamental addition to a basic structure that can stand well enough by itself. Rather, the microtones are part of the essential character of the melodic lines, and any performance that omits or modifies them is unthinkable" (Reid 1977, 159). Composer Lois Vierk, who has used *gagaku*-inspired glissandi in her own work, concurs. "It isn't a decoration. There's always a musical phrase that's going from one point to the other point, and the glissando gets you there. . . . To me glissando includes all kinds of continuous smoothly changing sound, be it of pitch, timbre, intensity, or volume" (Oteri 2008).

Akiyoshi described to Feather (1977) the inspiration and method for mimicking *gagaku* glissando in a jazz orchestra. While working on "Sumi-e,"

> I lay down on a bed and I began to hear this traditional Japanese *gagaku* sound. It's a form of very close harmony; and I heard it with a melody in my mind, repeating and repeating, and this Japanese sound matched it very well, in my head . . .
>
> I had the idea of writing this sound for trumpets. . . . Years ago in Japan, I used to hear trumpet players doing a lot of note-bending, both upward and downward. You have to slide into and out of things, using the valves very carefully. (14)

In "Kogun," however, trumpets do not play glissandi. In addition to Tabackin's flute lead, they are played by the woodwind section, one trombone, and arguably the bass, which has sliding, falling figures (Figure 5.3). Akiyoshi again creates a characteristically unusual mèlange of woodwind sounds: to the alto saxophone, she adds alto clarinet and two soprano saxophones, instruments seldom used in jazz orchestras. For better or worse, the soprano's timbre has been vaguely described as "oriental," so perhaps it contributes to the Asian sound of the piece.

Akiyoshi's instructions on the score say, "Glissandi are to be played like slides in pitch—starting at the first pitch and sliding into the ending pitch." The intervals covered range from minor seconds to perfect fifths, the widest being in Takackin's flute melody. The glissando players are synced as close to perfectly

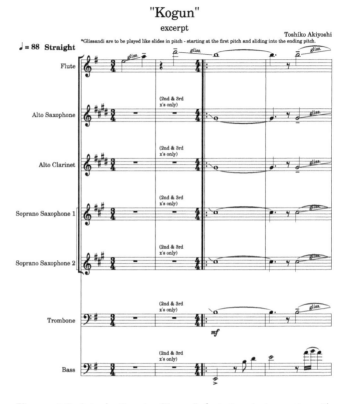

Figure 5.3: *Introduction to "Kogun," featuring instruments with glissandi. Excerpted from Akiyoshi 1979b.*

as possible; perhaps the *komi* (synchronization of breath) initiated by the *kakegoe* enables the glissando instruments to maintain balance between the intrinsic elasticity of the individual slides and ensemble cohesion.

Nevertheless, there is an inherent inexactitude in playing glissando that creates a wavering effect that could signify Onoda's liminality. Akiyoshi heightens that effect in two ways: by having the melismatic *kakegoe* vocals parallel the

Figure 5.3: *(Continued)*

horns; and by staggering the glissandi, adding specially timed variations in individual parts. In measure 5, all the glissando instruments play grace notes and scoops on beat three. In measure 10, the alto saxophone and soprano saxophone 1 each slides up a whole step from beats one to three, while on beat three the alto clarinet slides up chromatically a major second via eighth notes, and on beat four soprano saxophone 2 and trombone 1 slide up a major second via sixteenth notes.

Figure 5.3: *(Continued)*

These variations sonically suggest the vacillations in Onoda's mind as he tried, within his rigid ideological framework, to make sense of multiple messages telling him the war was over. I would argue they also depict the liminality of his experience as a bewildered warrior whose world had changed and left him behind (Figure 5.3).

* * *

Toshiko Akiyoshi described herself as a *kogun*. As a repatriate, she, too, occupied liminal space between imperial territory

Figure 5.3: *(Continued)*

(Manchuria) and metropole (Japan), both places in which her presence was unwelcome. She was a classically trained pianist with unusually deep exposure to *hōgaku* determined to master bebop, an immigrant in the United States, a woman in a male-dominated field, and an artist whose "authenticity" was questioned because of her race and nationality (Akiyoshi 2017, 21–3). Sometimes she believed that, as "a Japanese little girl trying to play jazz," her delusions were no less absurd than Onoda's.

Instead, she became a heroic figure who demonstrated that a Japanese could be admitted to a pantheon populated almost exclusively with Black and white American males, doing so with a judicious, well-conceived blend of native musical traditions and undiluted, hardcore jazz. Acclaim and acceptance did not mitigate or resolve her liminality; if anything, her liminality made her successes and exalted status in the jazz pantheon seem more remarkable. Having wryly titled a song "Warning! Success May be Hazardous to Your Health," Toshiko Akiyoshi long ago made peace with her positional ambiguity. Fortunately, the rest of the jazz world has, too.

* * *

Lew Tabackin cannot recall the exact date but thinks it may have happened in the 1980s. He and Akiyoshi were both in Japan, and he was scheduled to leave earlier. The day before his departure, she asked him to stay another day to join her for a show at Tokyo's Blue Note. She had just been informed that a special guest was coming to hear her that evening: Lt. Onoda Hiroo.

Akiyoshi asked her husband to play "Kogun" in a quartet setting. The moment was an incredible validation for his storytelling concept as an improvisor, while in a Zen "no-mind" (*mushin*) headspace.

> Him being there gave me a more inspiring narrative. And I really played, and I really got into it. He ran up on the stage and

he grabbed me. He was really excited. So that was a beautiful moment. Now that I thought of it, there are not that many beautiful moments—I hate to say that—but that was one of them. I felt like I really did it right, you know, I really told the story, and he was there to witness it. . . . I didn't get uptight. I just let it all happen. (2023)

Quoth Rahsaan Roland Kirk: "Bright moments," indeed.

6 The Reckoning

Nostalgia is a paralytic toxin.
GLEN WELDON, NPR, MAY 11, 2018

Kogun dropped in October 1974, seven months after Onoda Hiroo returned to Japan and during a period of intensified public discourse about the wartime past. *Kogun* appears to have been received as nothing more than a landmark jazz album, rather than a major artistic statement about history. The album title probably had no impact on its impressive sales, and neither Akiyoshi nor Isaka explicitly named Onoda in the Japanese release's sleeve notes; *Swing Journal* reviews and newspaper articles rarely mentioned Onoda, either. But his story was so widely known that audiences likely realized to whom the title alluded. However, in retrospect, "Kogun" (and, I would argue, "Memory") fits within a canon of artworks—consisting mostly of visual arts, literature, and cinema—that addressed modern Japan's darkest moments with greater directness than politicians, news media, and civil society were willing to muster.

The term "lone soldier" was not particularly arcane, but neither would it appear much in everyday speech. It is most often used in the phrase *kogun funtō*, a "forlorn struggle" in which one fights alone (or in a small unit) against a much larger force with no hope of reinforcements. Samurai heroes

Kusunoki Masashige (1294–1336) and Saigō Takamori (1828–77) are celebrated for courageously fighting and dying in *kogun funtō*. They are emblematic of what Japan scholar Ivan Morris (1975) called the "nobility of failure" (*kōki naru haiboku*): the ineluctability of their defeat "lends them a pathos which characterizes the general vanity of human endeavor and makes them the most loved and evocative of heroes" (xxii).

Akiyoshi's liner notes indicated its double meaning, referring also to her own personal, lonely (but ultimately victorious) *kogun funtō*: "My life playing jazz, the culture of a different country, seemed absurd and sad to me." Still, an album titled "lone soldier" released two years after Yokoi's reappearance, seven months after Onoda's, and two months before Nakamura's, certainly appeared timely. Besides the repatriation of the three castaways, other events and trends in the early 1970s were compelling more open discussion of the empire and war.

* * *

For decades now, news media outside of Japan have pushed a narrative that Japanese collectively have failed to acknowledge, much less atone for their nation's past military aggression and atrocities. Compared to Germany, which has made various high-profile efforts to take responsibility for Nazism and the Shoah, Japan always seems to fall short (Buruma 1994; Hein 2010).

This is true enough at the state level, for several reasons. The Japanese government has always insisted that all compensation issues were settled in the 1952 peace agreement and in a separate 1965 treaty with the Republic of

Korea, which is technically true. Under US military occupation after the Second World War, neither Japan nor Germany was pressured to engage in much sustained critical reflection that might inhibit economic and political recovery. American administrations deliberately scrubbed selected crimes from their ledgers, rehabilitated convicted war criminals, declined to prosecute others, and used ill-gotten science from the wartime regimes to gain advantages in the Cold War. In Japan, a small cabal of militarists was held responsible for the war, a perspective that encouraged the development of a "victim mentality" (*higaisha ishiki*) that absolved ordinary people (and the emperor) of war guilt (Hicks 1997, 17; Trefalt 2003, 9). The conservative Liberal Democratic Party, which has been in power most often since 1955, has thus mostly evaded public expressions of contrition and demands for recompense. Whereas Germany's Green Party has pushed for redress and reconciliation, Japanese who advocate similar efforts have no viable political representation or power (Hein 2010, 145; Seaton 2007, 36).

There are also high-profile, well-funded, politically connected organizations and individuals dedicated to minimizing or denying atrocities and promoting "patriotic education," including Nippon Kaigi and the Society for History Textbook Reform. Often described as "revisionist" (*shūsei-shugi*), they are better labeled "denialist" (*hitei-shuqi*): they minimize, justify, or deny outright the 1937 Nanjing Massacre, biological warfare research Unit 731, and the use of forced labor by colonial subjects and prisoners of war, while categorically dismissing the testimonies of hundreds of survivors involuntarily drafted into the so-called "comfort women" military prostitution system. Denialists may not represent the majority opinion, but they are loud and influential, capable of setting off diplomatic rows with Japan's neighbors.

Japan's alleged failure to address its imperialist past and wartime conduct with honesty, restitution, and genuine remorse has had major geopolitical consequences. It inhibits closer relations between Japan and South Korea, who can ill afford a rift with North Korea wantonly firing missiles about. To avoid angering some domestic constituencies, the apologies that *have* been issued are so carefully worded that they are typically dismissed as insincere. Random, ill-considered statements from public officials, middle-school textbooks, or civil society groups claiming that some well-documented war crime is a hoax are much more likely than statements of contrition to make headlines overseas.

Yet despite their high visibility, these right-wing nationalist views are not representative of the general public's attitudes. It is no fairer to say "the Japanese" have forgotten, ignored, or minimized their nation's history of military aggression than it is to say all "the Germans" have fully repudiated Nazism. "Rather than war history being an issue of national unity against an external other," Philip Seaton (2007) writes, "it has become an issue of national division along the lines of moral intuition and ideology" (36). That is, vigorous disputes about war responsibility and remembrance constitute one of the fundamental ideological cleavages in Japanese civil society and political culture.

* * *

The early 1970s witnessed the first major public reckoning since the early years of the US Occupation, prompted partly by the discovery of the three military castaways but also by various geopolitical events and the revelation of new evidence of wartime atrocities. By then, most of the population had been born after the war and, though curious about it, had no sympathy for the "cruder jingoism" of their forebears (Hicks 1997, 38). Pacifist education and antinuclear activism inspired by the Hiroshima and Nagasaki bombings had molded a generation averse to war, and the more they learned about it, the more they abhorred it.

Several factors inspired more critical historical reflection. One was the Vietnam War, in which Japan played a supporting role as a primary base from which American troops were deployed but which most of the public—especially university students—passionately opposed. In the late 1960s, Honda Katsuichi, an investigative reporter for the *Asahi Shinbun*, fed the fire with reports critical of American forces' conduct in Vietnam. In 1971, when Richard Nixon announced his intention to visit Beijing, Honda traveled to China to interview people about multiple Japanese military atrocities from the 1937–45 war, including the Nanjing Massacre. *Asahi* published his series of graphic testimonies, including horrific photographs, which were compiled into the book *Journey to China* (*Chūgoku no tabi*) in 1972. Honda eviscerated Japan's "reactionary government" and the press for decades of silence and for fostering the victim mentality that privileged Japanese suffering over that of others. His reportage shocked the public, drawing both praise and condemnation, particularly from military veterans' groups. Ever since, he has lived under near-constant death threats (Honda 1999; Yoshida 2000, 79–84).

Critical reflection was also encouraged by court victories in 1970 and 1975 for historian Ienaga Saburō (1913–2002), who sued the Ministry of Education in 1965 for censoring a high school textbook in which he described the Nanjing Massacre and other wartime atrocities. Many schoolteachers were inspired by Honda and Ienaga to conduct their own research about the war and teach it to their students (Yoshida 2000, 84). The Japan Teachers Union has been one of the most stalwart opponents of efforts by the government and right-wing organizations to whitewash this history.

In 1973, writer Senda Natsumitsu (1924–2000) published the first book on the "comfort women" system, relying primarily on interviews with veterans who had availed themselves of it. The following year, Tōei Studios released a love story based on Senda's book. Although this atrocity did not become widely known until Kim Hak-sun's (1924–97) public testimony in August 1991, Senda's book is considered the pioneer study in the field.

The reversion of Okinawa to Japanese sovereignty in 1972 provided another occasion for critical war remembrance. Okinawa lost at least a quarter of its population during nearly three months of brutal combat in 1945, many at the hands of the IJA, which allegedly ordered hundreds to commit "group suicides" (yet another subject the Ministry of Education ordered stricken from school textbooks in 2007). A prefectural history published in 1971 included personal testimonies from survivors about the cruelty of the army that was purportedly there to protect them from the Allied invasion (Hicks 1997, 41; Seaton 2007, 48).

Yet another catalyst was the flamboyant suicide by *seppuku* of acclaimed author Mishima Yukio (1925–70), the culmination of his personal crusade to resurrect the wartime virtues of martial masculinity and reverence for the emperor. A right-wing nationalist whose critiques of postwar Japan's materialism, spiritual vacuity, and dependency on the United States in fact mirrored those of leftist student activists, he nonetheless feared their unrest portended a communist revolution. On November 25, 1970, Mishima and four associates entered Camp Ichigaya, a Self-Defense Forces base, tied up its commandant, and admonished the jeering troops to stage a coup and reinstate military government. "Where has the spirit of the samurai gone?" he berated them. "Are you *bushi* [warriors]? Are you men?" He then disemboweled himself, which seemed to be his main objective anyway.

Those who saw "the nobility of failure" in Mishima's grisly deed were inspired to create the Issuikai, one of Japan's most venerable neo-nationalist organizations; but most people considered it a pathetic, self-indulgent stunt by a death-obsessed narcissist to revive an antidemocratic, militaristic value system (Seidensticker 1971; Yamanouchi 1972; McAdams 1985; Hicks, 1997, 31–3). Very few Japanese were impressed by gratuitous gut-slicing anymore.

* * *

Before this flurry of revelation and debate in the early 1970s, such direct confrontation with historical realities had been scattered. However, creative artists had hardly been reticent to address the war. Takeyama Michio's bestselling children's book *Harp of Burma* (1946) was made into a popular film in 1956 by

Ichikawa Kon. Ōka Shōhei presented a much bleaker view of war in his 1951 novel *Fires on the Plain*, which Ichikawa also adapted for the cinema in 1959. So-called "reportage painters" protested the Cold War military alliance with the United States, which had placed Japan in a "purgatory between war and peace" (Hoaglund 2012, 2–3). This is not to mention the growing literary, cinematic, and visual corpus created about and by survivors of the atomic attacks (*hibakusha*) from the 1950s.

If we consider *Kogun* a contribution to this corpus, the title track and "Memory" mark the debut of Toshiko Akiyoshi the Historian, the first in a series of compositions through which she presented critical perspectives on Japan's modern history by foregrounding the experiences of those who had suffered most. She repeatedly stated her intent to generate awareness and provoke forthright contemplation on historical and social issues.

> As a person in society, I have concerns about what happens in society. If I were a journalist, I would express this in writing, but I think I express it in the same way through music. Certainly, musicians can't change the world. That doesn't mean I want to remain silent. Through music, I say, "This is what I think. This is how I desire it to be," and I believe there is meaning in making a small ripple in a pond.[1]

The previous two chapters argued that "Memory" and "Kogun" are both pointed critiques of how individuals and societies remember and narrate the past. Memories do not simply sit around in our minds; they are *(re)made* by those who remember, to make the past present. The notion that individual and collective memories are proactively created, selected, modified, erased, and concealed to suit present circumstances is a foundational premise in the academic field of "memory studies," which has influenced various disciplines in the humanities and natural and social sciences. Akiyoshi's compositions are less about the tricks memory plays on us than about the tricks we play on memory. The genius of "staging" Onoda Hiroo's story as a *nō* play in the warrior and insanity genres was to highlight the delusory states (induced by fascist/militarist ideology) that inform not just present actions but also recollection. Even if *Kogun* itself did not figure prominently in the early 1970s' reckoning with wartime history, retroactively, we can see it as one of many artistic contributions to that discussion, inspired by one of the major events that prompted that reckoning in the first place.

Akiyoshi continued this project throughout her career as a composer and bandleader, creating a body of historically themed programmatic work that far exceeds that of her primary inspirations, Ellington and Mingus. According to Tabackin,

> About half the music she is writing deals with something outside of the music itself, and tries to musically tell a story. This seems to go in cycles in her writing. She will work on a story concept and create an extended musical work, such as "Minamata," followed by what we call "relief" pieces—shorter, "lighter" pieces that do not have a poetic storyline. As a player, I have often asked Toshiko to tell me as much as possible about the story concepts of her larger works, so that I could come

up with the right kinds of musical interpretations as a player. (Koplewitz 1991, 274)

It is beyond the purview of this book to go into depth about her later compositions on historical issues, but here are a few that interested readers can seek out.

- "Tales of a Courtesan" (*Tales of a Courtesan/Oirantan*, 1976): about the sale of daughters into prostitution during the Edo period. "What I tried to express was this contrast between being a cultured woman [*tayū*], leading what was superficially a very gay and luxurious life, while actually suffering from a tragic denial of human rights" (liner notes).

- *Minamata* suite (*Insights*, 1978): requiem for victims of the poisoning of a fishing village by the Chisso corporation, which dumped methylmercury into the sea. It "sears the soul . . . , a powerful elegy for the dead, maimed, blind and brain-damaged victims of the environmental disaster that ravaged the once idyllic Japanese fishing and farming village of Minamata."[2]

- "Two Faces of a Nation" (*European Memoirs*, 1983): impressions of the legacies of Nazism and war in Germany. "The charm of these picturesque towns and the warmth of the people conjured up visions of an old, innocent, carefree Germany. How in this setting could events have taken such a tragic, inhuman turn? . . . All nations have potential for great achievements, but also for incredible evil" (liner notes).

- *Kourakan* Suite (*Carnegie Hall Concert*, 1992): a "multicultural" composition commissioned by Fukuoka City to commemorate the archaeological discovery of Tsukushi Kōrokan in 1987, a guest house accommodating Chinese, Korean, and Near Eastern visitors traveling the Silk Road from the eighth to the twelfth centuries.

- *Hiroshima: Rising from the Abyss* suite (2002): requiem for victims of the atomic bombing. "This music represents an anti-nuclear weapon . . . and anti-war sentiment. No matter how hopeless the situation, we must have hope" (liner notes). By featuring Won Jang-Hyun on *taegŭm* (a transverse bamboo flute with a vibrating membrane), Akiyoshi drew specific attention to the oft-overlooked thousands of Koreans who perished.

Music intended for commemoration and memorialization often reinforces historical narratives endorsed by the powerful. Yet even when writing with commissions from municipal governments or arts institutions, Akiyoshi has presented counter-narratives focused on those who have borne the heaviest burdens, made the greatest sacrifices, and suffered the worst consequences of decisions and events not of their own making. That is how she viewed Onoda Hiroo when dedicating "Kogun" to him: though an extreme example, he represented a generation of people who devoted and lost their lives, literally or figuratively, in service to an ideological cause built on delusions, hubris, and violence.

Epilogue
The Legacy

I think we did pretty well, considering we had a band for 30 years. We did some really great things. You know, we made a contribution. How many people can actually feel that they've made a contribution?
LEW TABACKIN, NPR, FEBRUARY 16, 2016

Kogun has been out of print in North America and Europe for decades. It is reissued periodically in Japan (Sony Music Entertainment now owns the RCA/Victor catalog), most recently in 2019. In 2008, Mosaic Records issued a limited-edition, three-CD compilation of five TA-LTBB RCA studio albums as volume 33 in its Mosaic Select series. To my knowledge, that was the last time *Kogun* and the subsequent albums were made available outside of Japan. "We got some bread," Tabackin acknowledges. "I said, 'Well, Michael [Cuscuna], what about the shit that's never been released [in the United States] and that was recorded really well?' We were a phenomenon in the seventies and forget about the eighties or nineties. . . . As the Japanese say, 'Nothing comes in perfect form.'"

The live *Road Time* (1976), featuring a more authoritative performance of "Kogun" with onstage *tsuzumi* drumming by Katada Kisaku III (1935–2020) and Yazaki Yutaka, was reissued once on CD in Japan in 2006 (this live version appeared once on CD in the United States on a Novus Series '70 compilation from 1991). At this writing, major streaming services only carry a handful of Akiyoshi's 1950s–1960s small-group recordings, making YouTube the best place to hear the original TA-LTBB albums.

As is often the case, however, the significance of the music cannot be judged by the (un)availability of the original recordings. *Kogun* is most momentous for launching the career of Toshiko Akiyoshi as a composer, arranger, and bandleader. It presents an artist with a fully formed concept that she would continue to pursue and develop over subsequent decades. "*Kogun* was a gateway," Tabackin (2023) declares. "It was a phenomenon. It was not supposed to do anything. It had no money, no budget. It wasn't supposed to sell. And it just took off. . . . From Toshiko's point of view, it was the beginning, the foundation for her work. . . . Toshiko says her heritage was a negative; she turned a negative into a positive."

Kogun introduced all her signature traits: orchestral combinations creating unique tonal colors and harmonies, particularly in the woodwinds; idiosyncratic placement of accents in her arrangements; a bebop sensibility favoring vertical harmony, labyrinthine ensemble passages, and space for soloists; pieces written for specific individuals in the band; an experimental ethos, illustrated on *Kogun* with manual analog sequencing using prerecorded audio and studio effects; incorporation of Japanese musical elements, both subtle and prominent (in later work she drew on many other traditions), while carefully preserving what she considered the core essence of jazz (which she and Tabackin define as "a little bebop sensibility, a little blues sensibility") (Westbrook 2011,

307); and programmatic compositions that tell stories and provoke critical reflection on social issues and history.

Even among the small handful of ensembles performing new work, trying novel orchestral combinations, and otherwise demonstrating that the jazz big band was still a vibrant creative force and not just a vehicle for "yesteryear" nostalgia, the TA-LTBB stood out. Its rise to the top of the big band category in the *Down Beat* Readers and Critics polls—and Akiyoshi's rankings in the arranger and composer categories—was nothing short of meteoric. She became the "triple-crown queen," winning all three categories in the 1980 Readers Poll, a feat she duplicated in the 1982 Critics Poll.[1]

The composition "Kogun" was hardly the first successful effort to broaden the jazz vocabulary but was nevertheless a noteworthy step in the idiom's globalization. Akiyoshi determined that adding touches of *japonaiserie* would be the best way she could contribute something to the music, while harboring no expectations that "it could be a main influence in future jazz."

> But I decided that it's never going to be that—not in the way that Brazilian music, for instance, is a main influence today. You could almost say that Brazilian music changed the whole jazz scene. But I don't think it could ever happen that way [with Japanese music]. It's more of a special effect. (Feather 1977, 15)

However, if not Japanese music specifically, Asian musical traditions generally have had an impact on the jazz tradition: since the 1960s, many artists have been inspired by scales and modes, rhythms, instrumentation, repertoire, and aesthetic philosophies from beyond its principal sources in African

America. Akiyoshi was one of several high-profile artists—including Dave Brubeck, Alice and John Coltrane, Joe Harriott, Pharoah Sanders, and Don Cherry—who expanded and enriched the jazz palette without diluting the idiom's essence.

Even in this context, Akiyoshi's work is distinctive because of the depth of her roots in and knowledge of specific alternative music traditions. She was no dilettante. Integrating *nō* and *gagaku* was a far bolder, more complex endeavor than playing *min'yō* on jazz instruments or improvising using *raga* scales. "It has to be integrated to the point that it *all* sounds together. . . . If you infuse an element and it just remains something else," she's said, it will sound "very superficial" (Minor 2004, 38).

Akiyoshi is widely revered, but female and Asian American jazz artists, in particular, credit her with creating space for them. "She doesn't realize the impact that she had on them. I can't convince her," Tabackin sighs. "Ms. Akiyoshi is my role model as an Asian immigrant making an original contribution that reflected our heritage to the music both as a performer and composer," tenor saxophonist, composer, and cofounder of Asian Improv aRts Francis Wong testifies. "As a teenager I and my brothers listened to *Kogun* over and over again." Wong is representative of jazz artists of Asian heritage whose identities, like Akiyoshi's, were shaped by African American music but who were also inspired and emboldened by her example to integrate elements from various Asian musical traditions into their work. The music of Jon Jang, Fred Ho, Glenn Horiuchi, Jen Shyu, Vijay Iyer, and Susie Ibarra, among others, demonstrates the "'hybridity' of Asian American culture" (Kajikawa 2012; see also Fellezs 2007), analogous to the "blend" Akiyoshi created. Although these artists had more overt political agendas, they shared her concern with historical and social issues affecting minoritized and marginalized peoples.

* * *

After years of frustration with the lack of opportunities to play jazz in Los Angeles (Feather 1978a, 42), Tabackin persuaded Akiyoshi to return to New York in 1982 (Cho's documentary shows them packing for the move). She explained her assent:

> Everybody knows Lew is ten years younger than I am. Consequently, he started late. I came at a very good time. The old jazz clubs were all over the place, and they would hire me and hire everybody else. . . . Lew didn't have that. When he came out, jazz clubs were gone; just a few existed. . . . I think the main thing for me is to make better conditions or surroundings musically for him to be. Anything I can do, I do. Which is unfortunately not that much. (Kelly 2013, 240)

With their departure, the West Coast edition of the TA-LTBB ended. *European Memoirs* was its last recording.

The couple wasted little time assembling a "'New' New York Band" of mostly full-time jazz musicians, which debuted at Carnegie Hall on June 25, 1983, as part of the Kool Jazz Festival. Critic John Wilson wrote, "This new band already has the crisp, vital attack that was characteristic of its West Coast counterpart and a potential pool of interesting soloists to join Mr. Tabackin's flute and tenor saxophone."[2] Eventually rechristened the Toshiko Akiyoshi Jazz Orchestra featuring Lew Tabackin, the New York band continued with relatively stable personnel (and a "bench" of subs) for twenty more years.

Akiyoshi wrote increasingly grand, *Minamata*-scale suites for this ensemble. That is what most inspired jazz composer Maria Schneider, who saw the group in Minneapolis as a college student.

> The music was so beautiful, and there was something about it being displayed in that concert hall—and her conducting and her playing—just the whole took me.... It wasn't that she was a woman, but it was that somebody was doing jazz that was infused with classical—it was concert music.[3]

In 1996, the orchestra started a seven-year run of Monday night shows at Birdland but had little other work besides occasional trips to Japan. In 2003, she lamented that no American company had released its recordings since 1994's *Desert Lady Fantasy*, the second of two highly acclaimed albums on the high-profile Columbia label.

> Since then, we have three recordings for BMG Japan [*Four Seasons of Morita Village*, *Monopoly Game*, and *Tribute to Duke Ellington*], but BMG America never picked them up.... The main thing for me is it affects our job. This year, we have our thirtieth anniversary and so this year there are some things. Last year, we didn't have anything. I looked at the books in January. I, myself, was busy doing this and that and I didn't realize that the band did not have any job outside of Birdland, except one job in Japan. That was it. (AAJ Staff 2003b)

"The sad part of the whole big band, Toshiko Akiyoshi orchestra, whatever you want to call it," Tabackin reflects, "is that we managed to survive without any real help. We could've done better and reached more people. Again, very little distribution in Europe. We have about ten albums that never came out, outside of Japan."

The loyalty and commitment of the musicians under such circumstances are noteworthy. "People are doing other things to support themselves, but they give us a priority," Tabackin said of the NYC band. "They arrange their schedules to play in the band." Akiyoshi added, "After the Hiroshima concert, a couple of guys in the band said that they were proud to be in this organization. Musicians don't usually say things like that, but I like to think everybody felt like that."[4]

With some sadness and some relief, they disbanded the orchestra at the end of 2003, and with characteristic modesty, Akiyoshi said she needed to spend more time practicing piano.

Toshiko Akiyoshi has earned many accolades: *Swing Journal*'s inaugural Nanrio Fumio Prize (1976); fourteen Grammy nominations; numerous *Down Beat* critics' and readers' polls for composer, arranger, and big band; one *Swing Journal* Gold Disc (*Insights*, 1978) and two Silver Discs (*Kogun* and *Farewell*, 1981); *Down Beat* Jazz Album of the Year (*Insights*); New York City's Liberty Medal (1986); Ellis Island Medal of Honor (1986); two awards from the emperor of Japan, the Medal of Honor, Purple Ribbon (Shijuhōshō, 1997) and Order of the Rising Sun, Gold Rays with Rosette (Kyokujitsu Shōjushō, 2004); Japan Foundation Award (2004); and the BNY Mellon Living Legacy Award from the Mid-Atlantic Arts Foundation (2018). In March 2023, the Jazz at Lincoln Center Orchestra performed her music as part of a long-overdue two-day homage.[5] Yet no recognition means more to her than being named a National

Endowment for the Arts Jazz Master in 2007 (she was the third foreign-born recipient, after Marian McPartland and Paquito D'Rivera).

As the principal soloist in her orchestra, Lew Tabackin reached a larger audience than he might have as a solo artist, but he was also indispensable to Akiyoshi's sound and success. Still, one reason their musical and personal partnership has worked so well for over half a century is because each also pursues separate projects. Though often "lumped together" (Harrington 1980), Tabackin has said,

> We try to keep our specialties separate and try not to get in each other's way. If we both were writers, maybe we'd have this constant disagreement o[r] whatever. But we fulfill our own little spheres. . . . I'm in my little world and she's in hers. . . . We have a big enough space: I'm in the basement and she's two floors above. (Cerra 2013)

A glance at his Facebook page indicates that Tabackin maintains a busy performance schedule as a solo artist in New York and frequently tours Europe and Japan. Japanese audiences, in particular, have warmly embraced him. They respect and appreciate his immersion in and reverence for their culture and music, for much the same reason that so many Japanese effusively praise us foreigners for saying "Good morning" correctly: they appreciate the *effort* as much or more than the results. He regularly tours Japan with his longstanding trio (drummer Mark Taylor and bassist Boris Kozlov), records for Japanese record labels, and has been invited to perform flute improvisations at Zen temples and gardens—check out his performances at Fugetsuro Garden (2015) and Sengen Shrine in Shizuoka (2019) on YouTube (see Levy 2016).⁶

* * *

In *Blue Nippon*, I characterized the history of jazz in Japan as a century-long quest to authenticate (*seitōka*) indigenous jazz performance. Burdened with an "authenticity complex," jazz performers presumed their music was inferior to and less genuine than that performed by (African) Americans.

Figure 7.1: *Lew Tabackin and National Endowment for the Arts Jazz Master Toshiko Akiyoshi at the reception for 2007 NEA honorees, thirty-fourth Annual International Association for Jazz Education meeting in New York, January 12, 2007. Alamy Images.*

Toshiko Akiyoshi's *kogun funtō*—her forlorn struggle—was to overcome this angst, to contribute something to the idiom that no one else had or could.

In the 2020s, it appears that, although not entirely absent, the authenticity complex is less prominent or debilitating than it used to be. There are many probable reasons for this, not the least of which is the widespread acceptance of Japanese artists within the global "jazz diaspora" (Johnson 2019). As a pianist, composer, arranger, and bandleader, Toshiko Akiyoshi almost singlehandedly demolished assumptions that Japanese were mere imitators. Like any serious second-language learner, immersion empowered her to express herself, authentically and originally. Jazz became her native language.

Notes

Introduction

1 See her performance of "The Village" on French television at https://youtu.be/AElsKE48Gac. She describes the genesis of this "signature" piece in Akiyoshi 2017, 94–9.

Chapter 1

1 Igarashi (2016) writes that Onoda portrayed himself as an "elite officer entrusted with special missions, though in reality he was only one of the many warrant officers that the army hastily churned out" (175).

2 Different sources give Nakamura's Amis name as Shiniyuwu, Suniyon, or Attun Palalin. When the Nationalist government forced indigenous Taiwanese to adopt Chinese names, he became Li Guanghui.

3 Mutō was one of seven men convicted as Class-A war criminals by the International Military Tribunal for the Far East and hanged in December 1948, for his role in the 1937 Nanjing and 1945 Manila massacres.

4 Taniguchi had identified himself as Onoda's immediate superior in a newspaper interview, since his actual commander, Lt. General Yokoyama Shizuo (1890–1961) (Onoda 1974, 201, 213), had died. Yokoyama was tried and convicted as a war criminal for mass murders and rapes committed during the February 1945 Battle of Manila. He was pardoned in 1953.

5 Depending on the characters used, *donkō* could either mean "slow train" or "dull hook." However, Yoshikuni Igarashi speculates that *donkō* was either "a common epithet widely used by his contemporaries or one that Onoda made up in Lubang. But it is probably a combination of *dojin* [native] and *bankō* [barbarian], the latter of which appears in *Bōken Dankichi*," a wartime comic about a boy who conquers the natives of an unnamed South Pacific island (email correspondence, July 13, 2023).

Chapter 2

1 *DB*, September 9, 1949: 9.

2 *What's My Line?* (1956), season 7, episode 12, March 18, YouTube, https://youtu.be/7BRGccMFL4E.

3 The following biographical portrait is compiled from multiple sources: Akiyoshi 1996, 2008, 2017; Cho 1983; Honda 1984; Zen'on 2004; Moore 2004; Kelly 2013; Ogawa 2015; and Nishida 2019.

4 Akiyoshi reunited with Yang when she returned to Manchuria for the NHK television program *Trip to Where the Heart Belongs* (*Sekai waga kokoro no tabi*, broadcast October 17, 1993). Yang had been banished to a farm for "reeducation" during China's Cultural Revolution (1966–76), presumably for his connections to Japan and for playing a "bourgeois" instrument (see Kraus 1989).

5 Likely either Brunswick 7520 (recorded 1935) or Columbia 35711 (1939).

6 De Coteaux (1929–2005) wrote the strings arrangement for B.B. King's 1969 hit "The Thrill is Gone" and produced for Sister Sledge, Ben E. King, Marlena Shaw, and The Manhattans. In 1975 he released the instrumental album *A Stevie Wonder Songbook* (RCA ANL1-0923).

7 Likely from the 10" album *Piano Solos* (Mercury C-507, 1952), with Max Roach and Curly Russell.

8 *NYT*, October 1 and 9, 1967. Manuscripts from Mingus' 1962 recital (released on CD as *The Complete Town Hall Concert*, Blue Note 7243, 1994) were discovered and painstakingly reconstructed to create the monumental *Epitaph* suite. It was performed and recorded live by a thirty-piece all-star orchestra in 1989, and released on Columbia Records (CK2-45428, 1990).

Chapter 3

1 *LAT*, February 14, 1974: IV, 18.

2 *LAT*, May 27, 1974: IV, 13.

Chapter 4

1 *DB*, April 22, 1976: 24.

2 See "Kakaa Denka," https://worldheritage.pref.gunma.jp/; and "Kakaadenka," Japan Heritage Portal Site, https://japan-heritage.bunka.go.jp/ja/stories/story002/. A statue paying tribute to the breadwinning mother stands in front of the History and Folklore Museum in Kanra (possibly the village Feather mentioned in the liner notes) (see https://www.town.kanra.lg.jp).

3   I have not had access to European jazz periodicals' reviews of *Kogun*.

4   *SJ*, October 1974: 126.

5   *SJ*, February 1975: 123.

6   *AS*, November 29, 1974: 7.

7   *MS*, November 22, 1974: 9.

Chapter 5

1   *DB*, November 17, 1954: 14.

2   *DB*, March 21, 1956: 13.

3   Incidentally, the original recording of "Suzhou Nights" was voiced by another Manchuria-born Japanese entertainer, actress Yamaguchi Yoshiko (1920–2014), who spoke native Mandarin. The Manchurian Film Association kept her Japanese identity secret and presented her to audiences as an exemplary Chinese Japanophile named Li Xianglian (Jp: Ri Kōran).

4   See *Sugii Kōichi saron myūjikku*, 2CDs, King/Bridge 123/124, 2009.

5   Tabackin bought a *shakuhachi*, but "I couldn't find [the] right position of the embouchure hole, to direct the air. . . . When I tried to play it, it messed up my flute embouchure" (email correspondence, July 13, 2023).

6   Quoted in Chris Albertson's liner notes for *Desert Lady Fantasy*.

Chapter 6

1 *YS*, March 10, 2022, https://www.yomiuri.co.jp/column/japanesejazz/20220203-OYT8T50008/.
2 *Hartford Courant*, January 30, 1993, https://www.courant.com/1993/01/30/homage-to-minamata-sears-the-soul/.

Epilogue

1 *DB* December 1980: 17; and August 1982: 18.
2 *NYT*, June 27, 1983: C11.
3 NPR, February 16, 2016, https://www.npr.org/2016/02/16/466930497/toshiko-akiyoshis-jazz-orchestra-brought-the-club-to-concert-halls.
4 *DB*, July 2003: 47.
5 The Music of Toshiko Akiyoshi, March 10–11, Jazz at Lincoln Center, https://2023.jazz.org/music-of-toshiko-akiyoshi.
6 "Lew Tabackin Trio Stage on the water at Fugetsuro" (September 15, 2015), YouTube, https://youtu.be/_phepAkVWK0; and "LEW TABACKIN LIVE in 静岡浅間神社" (September 12, 2019), YouTube, https://youtu.be/tQNE3hlIAXc.

References

Abbreviations

AS = Asahi Shinbun
DB = Down Beat
LAT = Los Angeles Times
MS = Mainichi Shinbun
NPR = National Public Radio
NYT = New York Times
SJ = Swing Journal
YS = Yomiuri Shinbun

"#13 Toshiko Akiyoshi" (2012), J-Collabo.org, https://www.j-collabo.org/single-post/2012/08/29/13-toshiko-akiyoshi.

AAJ Staff (2003a), "A Fireside Chat with Lew Tabackin," All About Jazz, April 4, https://www.allaboutjazz.com/a-fireside-chat-with-lew-tabackin-lew-tabackin-by-aaj-staff.

AAJ Staff (2003b), "A Fireside Chat with Toshiko Akiyoshi," All About Jazz, April 20, https://www.allaboutjazz.com/a-fireside-chat-with-toshiko-akiyoshi-toshiko-akiyoshi-by-aaj-staff.

Akiyoshi, Toshiko (1960), *Jazz Originals for Any Solo Instrument or Combo*, Boston: Berklee Press.

Akiyoshi, Toshiko (1979a), "American Ballad," score for full jazz ensemble, Delevan: Kendor Music.

Akiyoshi, Toshiko (1979b), "Kogun," score for full jazz ensemble, Delevan: Kendor Music.

Akiyoshi, Toshiko (1979c), "My Elegy," score for full jazz ensemble, Delevan: Kendor Music.

Akiyoshi, Toshiko (1996), *Jazu to ikiru*, Tokyo: Iwanami Shinsho.

Akiyoshi, Toshiko (2008), interview with Anthony Brown, June 29–30, transcribed by E. Taylor Atkins, Smithsonian Jazz Oral History Program, National Museum of American History, https://americanhistory.si.edu/smithsonian-jazz/collections-and-archives/smithsonian-jazz-oral-history-program#Akiyoshi.

Akiyoshi, Toshiko (2017), *Endoresu janī: owari no nai tabi*, Tokyo: Shodensha, 2017.

Anno, Mariko (2020), *Piercing the Structure of Tradition: Flute Performance, Continuity, and Freedom in the Music of Noh Drama*, Ithaca: Cornell University Press.

Atkins, E. Taylor (2001), *Blue Nippon: Authenticating Jazz in Japan*, Durham: Duke University Press.

Atkins, E. Taylor (2018), "Frenemy Music? Jazz and the Aural Imaginary in Wartime Japan," *Memoria e Ricerca: Rivista di storia contemporanea* 26 (May–August): 241–60.

Bohlman, Philip, and Goffredo Plastino, eds. (2016), *Jazz Worlds/World Jazz*, Chicago: University of Chicago Press.

Buckley, Roger, and Tamara Roberts (2013), *Yellow Power, Yellow Soul: The Radical Art of Fred Ho*, Urbana: University of Illinois Press.

Buruma, Ian (1994), *The Wages of Guilt: Memories of War in Germany and Japan*, New York: Meridian.

Cerra, Steve (2013), "Toshiko Akiyoshi: Traditionalist and Innovator," JazzProfiles, https://jazzprofiles.blogspot.com/2013/11/toshiko-akiyoshi-traditionalist-and.html.

Cho, Renee, dir. (1983), *Jazz is My Native Language: A Portrait of Toshiko Akiyoshi, Rhapsody Films*, VHS.

Crouch, Stanley (2000), "The Genres: Stanley Crouch on Mainstream," *Jazz Times* (September), https://jazztimes.com/features/columns/the-genres-stanley-crouch-on-mainstream/.

DeVeaux, Scott (1997), *The Birth of Bebop: A Social and Musical History*, Berkeley: University of California Press.

Echigoya, Kōji (1992), *Bōkenka no tamashii: Onoda shōi hakkensha Suzuki Norio no shōgai*, Tokyo: Kōfusha Shuppan.

Esslin, Martin (1960), "The Theatre of the Absurd," *Tulane Drama Review* 4 (May): 3–15.

Feather, Leonard (1976), "East Meets West, or Never the Twain Shall Cease: Toshiko Akiyoshi and Lew Tabackin," *DB*, June 3: 16–17, 38–9.

Feather, Leonard (1977), "Toshiko Akiyoshi: Contemporary Sculptress of Sound," *DB*, October 20: 13–15, 44.

Feather, Leonard (1978a), "Lew Tabackin—Tabackin Road," *DB*, January 26: 14–16, 40, 42.

Feather, Leonard (1978b), "Toshiko Akiyoshi—The Leader of the Band," *Ms.*, 7 (November): 34–40.

Fellezs, Kevin (2007), "Silenced but Not Silent: Asian Americans and Jazz," in *Alien Encounters*, ed. Mimi Thi Nguyen, 70–108, Durham: Duke University Press.

Fellezs, Kevin (2010), "Deracinated Flower: Toshiko Akiyoshi's 'Trace in Jazz History,'" *Jazz Perspectives* 4 (April): 35–57.

Fujinami, Osamu (1977), "Rubangu-tō no izoku," *Shokun* (September): 117–37.

Fujita, Takanori (2019), "Layers and Elasticity in the Rhythm of Noh Songs: 'Taking Komi' and Its Social Background," in *Thought and Play in Musical Rhythm: Asian, African, and Euro-American Perspectives*, eds. Richard K. Wolf, Stephen Blum, and Christopher Hasty, 212–31, New York: Oxford University Press.

Gioia, Ted (2021), *The History of Jazz*, 3rd ed., New York: Oxford University Press.

Goto, Ken'ichi (2003), *Tensions of Empire: Japan and Southeast Asia in the Colonial and Postcolonial World*, Athens and Singapore: Ohio University Press and Singapore University Press.

Gourse, Leslie (1995), *Madame Jazz: Contemporary Women Instrumentalists*, New York: Oxford University Press.

Hancock, Herbie, with Lisa Dickey (2014), *Possibilities*, New York: Viking.

Harrington, Robert (1980), "The First Couple of Jazz," *Washington Post*, September 1, https://www.washingtonpost.com/archive/lifestyle/1980/09/01/the-first-couple-of-jazz/2a6dc759-4ce0-4c7b-b8b4-d36e1d24c7c2/.

Harris, George (2016), "Lew Tabackin's Soundscapes: Last of the Big-Toned Tenors," *Jazz Weekly*, October 1, https://www.jazzweekly.com/2016/10/lew-tabackins-soundscapes-last-of-the-big-toned-tenors/.

Hawes, Hampton, with Don Asher (1979), *Raise Up Off Me: A Portrait of Hampton Hawes*, New York: Da Capo Press.

Hayashi, Eiichi (2014). *Zanryū nipponhei: Ajia no ikita ichimannin no sengo*, Tokyo: Chūkō Shinsho, Kindle.

Hein, Patrick (2010), "Patterns of War Reconciliation in Japan and Germany, A Comparison," *East Asia* 27: 145–64

Hicks, George (1997), *Japan's War Memories: Amnesia or Concealment?* Aldershot: Ashgate.

Hoaglund, Linda (2012), "Protest Art in 1950s Japan: The Forgotten Reportage Painters," MIT Visualizing Cultures, https://visualizingcultures.mit.edu/protest_art_50s_japan/anp1_essay.pdf.

Honda, Katsuichi (1972), *Chūgoku no tabi*, Tokyo: Asahi Shinbunsha.

Honda, Katsuichi (1999), *The Nanjing Massacre: A Japanese Journalist Confronts Japan's National Shame*, ed. Frank Gibney, trans. Karen Sandness, Armonk: M.E. Sharpe.

Honda, Toshio (1984), *Rongu ierō rōdo: jazu sankan joō no nagai michi nori—Akiyoshi Toshiko*, Tokyo: Ikkōsha.

Hosokawa, Shūhei (2007), "'Nihonteki jazu' o megutte," *Nihon kenkyū* 35 (May 21): 451–67.

Igarashi, Yoshikuni (2000), *Bodies of Memory: Narratives of War in Postwar Japanese Culture, 1945-1970*, Princeton: Princeton University Press.

Igarashi, Yoshikuni (2016), *Homecomings: The Belated Return of Japan's Lost Soldiers*, New York: Columbia University Press.

Ishii, Mikiko (1994), "The Noh Theater: Mirror, Mask, and Madness," *Comparative Drama* 28 (Spring): 43–66.

Johnson, Bruce (2019), *Jazz Diaspora: Music and Globalisation*, London: Routledge.

Kajikawa, Loren (2012), "The Sound of Struggle: Black Revolutionary Nationalism and Asian American Jazz," in *Jazz/Not Jazz: The Music and Its Boundaries*, eds. David Ake, Charles Hiroshi Garrett, and Daniel Ira Goldmark, 190–216, Berkeley: University of California Press.

Kanze Ryū, https://kanze.net/en/.

Kelly, Jennifer (2013), *In Her Own Words: Conversations with Composers in the United States*, Urbana: University of Illinois Press.

Koplewitz, Laura (1991), "Toshiko Akiyoshi: Jazz Composer, Arranger, Pianist, and Conductor," in *The Musical Woman: An International Perspective*, vol. II, *1984-1985*, ed. Judith Lang Zaimont, 256–79, New York: Greenwood Press.

Kraus, Richard (1989), *Pianos and Politics in China: Middle-Class Ambitions and the Struggle Over Western Music*, New York: Oxford University Press.

Kunaichō (Imperial Household Agency), "*Gagaku* (Japanese Imperial Court Music and Dance)," https://www.kunaicho.go.jp/e-culture/gagaku.html.

Levy, Aidan (2016), "Overdue Ovation for Lew Tabackin: Virtuosity, Longevity, Productivity," *Jazz Times*, March 6, https://jazztimes.com/features/profiles/overdue-ovation-for-lew-tabackin/.

"Lew Tabackin Biography" (n.d.), Musician Guide, https://musicianguide.com/biographies/1608004052/Lew-Tabackin.html.

Manabe, Noriko (2013), "Representing Japan: 'National' Style Among Japanese Hip-Hop DJs," *Popular Music* 32, no. 1: 35–50.

McAdams, Dan (1985), "Fantasy and Reality in the Death of Yukio Mishima," *Biography* 8: 292–317.

Mercer, Michelle (2004), *Footprints: The Life and Work of Wayne Shorter*, New York: Tarcher/Penguin.

Minor, William (2004), *Jazz Journeys in Japan: The Heart Within*, Ann Arbor: University of Michigan Press.

Monterey Jazz Festival (2016), "Toshiko Akiyoshi and Terri Lyne Carrington: Musical Memories and Career Inspirations," SoundCloud, https://on.soundcloud.com/1QAkM.

Moore, Steven (2004), "The Art of Becoming a Jazz Musician: An Interview with Toshiko Akiyoshi," *Michigan Quarterly Review* 42 (Summer), http://hdl.handle.net/2027/spo.act2080.0043.307.

Morris, Ivan (1975), *The Nobility of Failure: Tragic Heroes in the History of Japan*, Tokyo: Tuttle.

Nishida, Hiroshi (2019), *Akiyoshi Toshiko to Watanabe Sadao*, Tokyo: Shinchosha.

Noh as Intermedia, https://noh.stanford.edu/music.

Ogawa, Takao (2015), *Shōgen de tsuzuru Nihon no jazu*, Tokyo: Komakusa Shuppan.

Omi, Hatashin (2009), *Private Yokoi's War and Life on Guam, 1944–1972: The Story of the Japanese Imperial Army's Longest*

WWII Survivor in the Field and Later Life, Folkestone, Kent: Global Oriental.

Onoda, Hiroo (1974), *No Surrender: My Thirty-Year War*, trans. Charles S. Terry, Tokyo: Kodansha.

Oteri, Frank (2008), "Lois V Vierk: Slideways," New Music USA, January 1, http://www.newmusicbox.org/articles/lois-v-vierk-slideways.

Perez, Mathieu (2016), "Lew Tabackin: Zen," *Jazz Hot* 675, https://www.jazzhot.net/PBCPPlayer.asp?ID=1735766.

Porter, Eric (2010), "Introduction: Rethinking Jazz Through the 1970s," *Jazz Perspectives* 4 (April): 1–5.

Priestly, Brian (1982), *Mingus: A Critical Biography*, New York: Da Capo Press.

Provine, Robert, Yoshihiko Tokumaru, and J. Lawrence Witzleben, eds. (2001), *The Garland Encyclopedia of World Music*, Volume 7: *East Asia: China, Japan, and Korea*, London: Routledge.

Reid, James (1977), review of *Music of a Thousand Autumns: The Tōgaku Style of Japanese Court Music* by Robert Garfias, *Journal of the American Musicological Society* 30 (Spring): 157–9.

Rikugunshō (1941), *Field Service Code (Senjinkun)—Adopted by the War Department on January 8, 1941, and translated into English by the* Tokyo Gazette, Tokyo: Tokyo Gazette Publishing House.

Rothbart, Peter (1980), "Toshiko Akiyoshi," *DB (August)*: 14–15, 62.

Saitō, Yuriko (2014), "Echigo kara Jōshū e watatta meshimori onna to 'Yagi bushi,'" *Meiji Gakuin University Annual Report of the Institute for International Studies* 17 (October): 31–43, http://hdl.handle.net/10723/2152.

Sankei Shinbun Fuji Terebi Tokubetsu Shuzaihan (1972), *The Last Japanese Soldier: Corporal Yokoi's 28 Incredible Years in the Guam Jungle*, trans. Ruri Corley Smith, London: Tom Stacey.

Santoro, Gene (2000), *Myself When I Am Real: The Life and Music of Charles Mingus*, Oxford: Oxford University Press.

Satō, Aiko (1987), *Suniyon no isshō*, Tokyo: Bungei Shunjū.

Seaton, Philip (2007). *Japan's Contested War Memories: The "Memory Rifts" in Historical Consciousness of World War II*, London: Routledge.

Seidensticker, Edward (1971), "Mishima Yukio," *Hudson Review* 24 (Summer): 272–82.

Sekine, Masaru (1985), *Ze-ami and His Theories of Noh Drama*, Gerrards Cross: Colin Smythe.

Shimazaki, Chifumi (1998), *Troubled Souls from Japanese Noh Plays of the Fourth Group*, Ithaca: East Asia Program, Cornell University.

Shoemaker, Bill (2018), *Jazz in the 1970s: Diverging Streams*, Lanham: Rowman & Littlefield.

Stewart, Alex (2007), *Making the Scene: Contemporary New York City Big Band Jazz*, Berkeley: University of California Press.

Stewart, Zan (1994), "A Gist Cause: Meaning—That's What It's All About for Toshiko Akiyoshi When It Comes to Her Music," *LAT*, December 3.

Stowe, David (2006), "Jazz That Eats Rice: Toshiko Akiyoshi's Roots Music," in *AfroAsian Encounters: Culture, History, Politics*, eds. Heike Raphael-Fernández and Shannon Steen, 277–94, New York: NYU Press.

Su, Kwang-ha (1975), "The Crossroads of Noh and the Theatre of the Absurd," *Asian Culture Quarterly* 3 (December): 52–6.

Suzuki, Norio (1974), *Daihōrō: Onoda shōi hakken no tabi*, Tokyo: Bungei Shunjū.

Swan, Annalyn (1980), "Jazz with Oriental Spice," *Newsweek*, July 14: 52B.

Tabackin, Lew (2000), *The Lew Tabackin Collection*, Milwaukee: Hal Leonard.

The-Noh.com, https://www.the-noh.com.

Toi, Jūgatsu (2005), *Onoda Hiroo no owaranai tatakai*, Tokyo: Shinchōsha.

"Toshiko Akiyoshi" (1998), *Jazz Profiles, NPR*, June 7.

Trefalt, Beatrice (2003), *Japanese Army Stragglers and Memories of the War, 1950–1975*, London: Routledge Curzon.

Tyler, Royall (1992), *Japanese Nō Dramas*, New York: Penguin.

Waley, Arthur (1921), *The Nō Plays of Japan*, London: Unwin.

Watt, Lori (2009), *When Empire Comes Home: Repatriation and Reintegration in Postwar Japan*, Cambridge, MA: Harvard University Press.

Westbrook, Peter (2011), *The Flute in Jazz: Window on World Music*, 2nd ed., Rockville: Harmonia Books.

Wong, Deborah (2004), *Speak It Louder: Asian Americans Making Music*, London: Routledge.

Yamakage, Kōfuku and Matsudo Rikio (1968), *Iōjima saigo no futari*, Tokyo: Yomiuri Shinbunsha.

Yamanouchi, Hisaaki (1972), "Mishima Yukio and His Suicide," *Modern Asian Studies* 6: 1–16.

Yasuda, Noboru (2021), *Noh as Living Art: Inside Japan's Oldest Theatrical Tradition*, trans. Kawamoto Nozomu, Tokyo: Japan Publishing Industry Foundation for Culture.

Yoshida, Takashi (2000), "A Battle Over History: The Nanjing Massacre in Japan," in *The Nanjing Massacre in History and Historiography*, ed. Joshua Fogel, 70–132, Berkeley: University of California Press, 2000.

Zen'on Gakufu Shuppansha (2004), *Kogun: Akiyoshi Toshiko—sono jinsei to sakuhin*, Tokyo: Zen'on Gakufu Shuppansha.

Interviews/email correspondence

Price, Mike (2023), Facebook Messenger, June 13.

Shew, Bobby (2023), Zoom, May 22.

Tabackin, Lew (2023), Zoom, January 16.

Wong, Francis (2023), email correspondence, July 13.

Select Discography
Toshiko Akiyoshi (Mariano):

Toshiko's Piano, 10" LP, Norgran MGM-22, 1954; released in Japan as *Amazing Toshiko Akiyoshi*.
The Toshiko Trio, LP, Storyville 912, 1956.
Toshiko Akiyoshi Recital, LP, Asahi Sonorama TAM YX-4056/King K28Y6219, 1961.
Toshiko Mariano Quartet, LP, Candid CS-9012, 1961.
Toshiko Mariano and Her Big Band, LP, Vee-Jay VJR-2505, 1964; released in Japan as *Toshiko and Modern Jazz*, Nippon Columbia PS-1126/30CY-1387.
Toshiko at Top of the Gate, LP, Nippon Columbia XMS-10008CT, 1986.
The Personal Aspect in Jazz, LP, CD4B-5007, 1971; reissued as *Sumie*, Victor SPX 1040, 1977.

Toshiko Akiyoshi-Lew Tabackin Big Band:

Road Time, 2 LPs, RCA Victor RVC 9115-9116, 1976.
European Memoirs, LP, Ascent ASC-1003, 1983.
Mosaic Select: Toshiko Akiyoshi-Lew Tabackin Big Band, 3 CDs, Mosaic Records MS-033, 2008. Contains the RCA/Victor albums *Kogun*, *Long Yellow Road*, *Tales of a Courtesan (Oirantan)*, *Insights*, and *March of the Tadpoles*.

Toshiko Akiyoshi Jazz Orchestra Featuring Lew Tabackin:

Wishing Peace, CD, Ken Music 27KEN-001, 1989.
Carnegie Hall Concert, CD, Columbia CK 48805, 1992

Desert Lady Fantasy, CD, Columbia CK 57856, 1994
Hiroshima: Rising from the Abyss, CD, True Life Jazz TE 1000082, 2002.

Lew Tabackin:

Dual Nature, LP, Inner City Records, IC-1028, 1978.
Rites of Pan, LP, Discomate DSP-5009, 1978.
Soundscapes, CD, independently released, 2015.

Index

Akatsu Yūichi   9, 10, 16
Akiyoshi, Toshiko
  acclaim, awards, and honors   3, 65, 96, 116–18
  early biography   25–39
  influence and contributions to jazz   25, 48, 69, 111, 113–14, 116
  as programmatic composer/storyteller   7, 23, 62, 72–3, 81, 85, 89, 96, 106–9, 113
  struggles of   1–5, 23, 37, 120
  stylistic characteristics of   60–1, 63, 77, 91, 107–9, 112–13
Akiyoshi Katsurō (father)   29, 68, 74
Asian American jazz   67–8, 114–15
atomic/nuclear weapons   103, 106, 109

Basie, Count   34, 43, 45, 46
Beppu   31, 37

Berklee School of Music   1, 27, 34, 35, 49, 69
big bands   4, 27, 40, 43–6, 65, 113. *See also* jazz
  and nostalgia   45, 113
Bley, Carla   4, 45
Boston   1, 27, 34, 49
Brazil   5, 18, 113
Buddhism   74, 83–4, 87
  Zen   75, 81, 96, 118–19
bushidō   6, 15, 83
Byard, Jaki   36

Calloway, Cab   39, 40
Chambers, Paul   1, 37
Cherico, Gene   36, 49, 58
Cherry, Don   36, 114
China   11, 14, 28–31, 70, 74, 89, 103, 122. *See also* Manchuria
Cold War   6, 101, 106
Coltrane, John   38, 39, 114
Cozy Quartet   25–7, 33, 34
Crouch, Stanley   46–7

Daugherty, Bob   47, 56

Davis, Miles 34, 46
Dolphy, Eric 41, 46
Donald, Peter 52–3, 58
Dorsey, Tommy 43, 45, 46
Down Beat 34, 44, 53, 58, 60, 65, 67, 113, 117

"Elegy" (composition; also known as "Toshiko's Elegy" and "My Elegy") 60, 65
Ellington, Duke 4, 7, 39, 43, 45, 46, 61, 63, 68, 70, 107, 116
Ellis, Don 45
emperor of Japan 6, 9, 10, 16, 21, 83, 88, 90, 101, 105, 117
European Memoirs (album) 108, 115
Evans, Gil 45, 53, 61

fascism 10, 15, 21, 22, 85–6, 107. *See also* militarism; Nazism
Feather, Leonard 52–3, 60–2, 64, 91, 124
Fukuoka 32, 109

gagaku (court music) 23, 41, 71–3, 89–91, 114
　glissandi 71, 72, 77, 78, 89–94
Germany 5, 69, 100–1, 108

Goodman, Benny 45
Granz, Norman 33–4

Hampton, Lionel 39, 45
Hara Nobuo 69
Hattori Ryōichi 68, 70
Hawes, Hampton 25, 27, 33
"Henpecked Old Man" (composition) 38, 50, 58, 63–4, 70
Herman, Woody 45
Hiroshima: Rising from the Abyss (suite) 82, 109, 117
Ho, Fred 67, 114
hōgaku (traditional Japanese music) 5, 30, 65, 68–70, 72, 75, 77, 79, 91, 95, 96, 112, 113
　folk songs (*min'yō*) 63–4, 69, 70
Honda Katsuichi 6, 103–4

Imperial Japanese Army (IJA) 9, 11, 17, 22, 104
Indonesia 14
Isaka Hiroshi 57, 99

jazz
　bebop 1, 4, 25–7, 33, 41, 60, 70, 78, 79, 95, 112
　fusion (jazz-rock/funk) 4, 47, 65

in the 1970s   4, 45–8
women in   3, 4, 35, 47, 64, 114
"world jazz"   3, 5, 36, 42, 113–14
jazz in Japan   25–7, 32, 37, 65, 67–9, 118–20
　authenticity of   23, 67–8, 95, 119–20
　dance halls   11, 26–7, 32, 33
　jazz coffeeshops (*jazu kissa*)   2, 27, 33

Katada Kisaku III   76, 111
Kenton, Stan   36, 45
Kirk, Rahsaan Roland   41, 97
Kogun (album)   3–6, 22–3, 57–66, 99, 100, 111–13, 117
　reviews of   58, 60, 65–6, 99, 124
"Kogun" (composition)   3, 6–7, 22–3, 30, 70–97, 99, 106, 109, 111, 113
kogun funtō (forlorn struggle)   23, 94–6, 99–100, 120
Korea   28, 31, 89, 100–2, 109
Kozuka Kinshichi   9, 16–19, 21, 22, 84, 86

Lateef, Yusef   36, 41

Lewis, John   48
"Long Yellow Road" (composition)   1, 3, 28, 52
Los Angeles   3, 25, 48, 53, 115
Lubang island. *See* Philippines

Manchuria   28–30, 95, 122, 124. *See also* China
Manne, Shelly   36, 52–3
Marcos, Ferdinand   29, 88
Mariano, Charlie   1, 36, 37, 60, 63
Mariano, Monday Michiru   1, 37
Marsalis, Wynton   46
"Memory" (composition)   61–2, 77, 99, 106–7
militarism   6, 10, 88, 101, 105, 107. *See also* fascism
Minamata (suite)   30, 82, 107, 108, 116
Mingus, Charles   1, 4, 7, 36–8, 40, 107, 123
Monterey Jazz Festival   48, 65
Moody, James   41, 78

Nakamura Teruo (Suniyon)   14, 21, 83–5, 87, 100, 121
National Endowment for the Arts Jazz Master award   119

Nazism 5, 31, 100, 102, 108. *See also* fascism; Germany
Newport Jazz Festival 34, 35, 69
New York 2, 25, 34, 38, 40, 41, 44, 45, 47–9, 115, 117–19
nōkan (bamboo flute) 41, 75, 76, 80
nō theater 23, 30, 41, 68, 72–8, 82–9, 107, 114
    Kanze school 74

Occupation of Japan 5, 6, 26, 32, 101, 103
Onoda Hiroo 3, 9–23, 72–3, 78, 82–9, 92, 94, 96, 99, 100, 107, 109, 121, 122
    meeting Akiyoshi and Tabackin 96–7
Ōsaka 48

Pettiford, Oscar 1, 26, 33
Philadelphia 34, 39, 40, 79
Philippines 3, 9, 14, 16–20, 22, 88
    Lubang island 9, 15–21, 23, 86, 88, 122
Powell, Bud 27, 33–5
Price, Mike 49, 57, 59

RCA/Victor 3, 57, 58, 61, 111

Road Time (live album) 58, 64, 76, 111
Roker, Mickey 1, 47
Rollins, Sonny 38, 40

Sano Tasuku 68–9
Schillinger Method 35–6
Schneider, Maria 4, 116
Second World War 3, 5, 6, 9, 11, 14, 15, 17, 18, 20–3, 30–1, 69, 70, 86–9, 94, 101, 103, 122
    remembrance of 5–7, 31, 99–105, 107
Segawa Masahisa 65
shakuhachi (end-blown bamboo flute) 41, 69, 78–80, 88, 124
Shew, Bobby 49–53, 57, 59, 61, 64
Shimada, Shōichi 9, 16–17, 84
Sugii Kōichi 68, 70, 124
Sun Ra 4, 45
Suzuki Norio 19–20
Swing Journal 65, 99, 117

Tabackin, Lew
    early biography 38–42
    as narrative/storytelling improvisor 78, 81–2, 96–7

stylistic characteristics of   40, 78–81, 91, 115, 118–19
Taiwan   14, 31, 84–5, 121
Tales of a Courtesan/Oirantan (album)   58, 108
Taniguchi Yoshimi   10, 17, 20, 121
Terry, Clark   38, 40
Thad Jones-Mel Lewis Orchestra   41, 45
Tokyo   17, 27, 30, 33, 37, 55, 63, 64, 66, 81, 96
Toshiko Akiyoshi Jazz Orchestra Featuring Lew Tabackin   115–16, 118
Toshiko Akiyoshi-Lew Tabackin Big Band (TA-LTBB)   22, 47, 52–4, 57–8, 76, 111–13, 115, 118
Toshiko at Top of the Gate (album)   41, 58
Toshiko's Piano (album; also known as *The Amazing Toshiko Akiyoshi*)   34, 67
Town Hall   36, 37, 40, 45, 48, 70, 123

Vietnam War   17, 103
"The Village" (composition)   1, 38, 50, 53, 70, 121

Watanabe Sadao   25, 36
Welding, Pete   60, 61, 63, 65
Wess, Frank   41, 78
Woodman, Britt   57, 60, 63

"Yagi Bushi" (folk song)   63–4, 70
Yamamoto Hōzan   69
Yazaki Yutaka   111
Yokohama   27, 33
Yokoi Shōichi   14, 20, 21, 83, 84, 87–8, 100
Yoshida Mamoru   33
Yui Shōichi   65–6

zanryū nipponhei (castaway soldiers)   13–15, 83–6, 100, 103. *See also* Nakamura Teruo; Onoda Hiroo; Yokoi Shōichi
Zeami Motokiyo   67, 74, 84–6

www.ingramcontent.com/pod-product-compliance
Ingram Content Group UK Ltd.
Pitfield, Milton Keynes, MK11 3LW, UK
UKHW030639220125
453959UK00002B/2